MW00425417

YOU DON'T KNOW WHAT YOU DON'T KNOW

Secrets Revealed from
a Health Insurance
Industry Insider!

FRANK STICHTER, MHP

CONTENTS

INTRODUCTION

MY JOURNEY IN THE INSURANCE business began shortly after graduating from college. I actually come from a family of attorneys— both grandfathers were attorneys, my father and four uncles were attorneys, and I had ambitions of going to law school. My father had always talked with me about selling, but in the sense of selling concepts and solving problems — selling intangibles, not tangible products per se. After four years of college, another three years of law school didn't really appeal to me so I entered the insurance business with Connecticut Mutual Life Insurance Company.

Prior to entering the life insurance business, you go through a number of different profile examinations. They are not aptitude examinations— they ask more attitude-type questions. The responses to those questions are modeled to closely match those of successful insurance people. I didn't do so well because I had a lack of knowledge about selling, the insurance business, and the business world. In fact, one of the profiles I took was with a sports psychologist who ultimately determined that my determination to succeed would overcome any deficiencies that were identified in the battery of examinations.

The General Agent of Connecticut Mutual at the time, Robert Meeker (a Hall of Famer in the insurance world) hired me for $440 a month and the balance of my compensation was to come from commissions through the life insurance and disability products that I would sell to my prospects and clients. At the end of the year, Connecticut Mutual found from my sales production that I could in fact sell insurance, and they then hired me as a full-time agent. Per my agreement with Bob, I was required to repay all the money that he had paid me during the previous year.

My prospects early in my career were those who had personal insurance needs. These were people that were recently married, had a new baby, some simple business needs, and some estate planning. Most of my meetings were around the kitchen table, usually in the evening, after numerous hours of dialing on the phone. I remember meeting with a couple who had two young children and who had no life insurance, and were reluctant to spend even $10 a month on a term life insurance policy.

Ultimately, they didn't buy any insurance and went uninsured. As I drove home that evening I thought, "What am I doing, banging my head against the wall, trying to convince people to buy any insurance when they see no need and don't want to spend $10 a month?" The point here is not the $10 a month to purchase insurance, it's that they thought they were doing just fine and didn't need to do anything different than what they were doing then.

They didn't know what they didn't know.

That was the end of my personal life insurance encounters, and I quickly moved into the group health insurance arena. I worked mainly with small groups with fewer than 100 lives who, at the time, were upset about the fact that they were getting 3% increases from Blue Cross Blue Shield. More and more insurance companies were getting into the health insurance marketplace and it was very competitive. There were no stringent regulations and mandatory benefits that individual States and the Feds have today, and the Employee Retirement and Income Security Act of 1974 (ERISA) had just come on the scene several years before. In fact, there were many things that employers could do with their insurance programs that would be deemed discriminatory today.

One time, I was asked to provide some insurance options for one of my father's clients, who had a large company of several hundred employees. This company was a magazine wholesaler located in four states in the Midwest. The owner of the company had a very good friend who was the current insurance agent. I was asked to provide some alternatives, and being young in my career, of course my alternatives were scrutinized by the current broker.

In the end, my program made financial sense — it was a partially self-funded program whereas the current program was fully insured. And while the termination of the relationship was awkward for the owner of the wholesaling company (my new client), over the years it was deemed to be the right solution. Every year, the current broker brought back an alternative to try to compete with it, but never could. This was back in the late

YOU DON'T KNOW WHAT YOU DON'T KNOW

1970s, and it was a new era for partial self-funding for groups under one thousand employees. Everyone believed that you had to be much larger to be partially self-funded, which was obviously not the case.

I began marketing this program with a particular Third Party Administrator (TPA) that had provided excellent service to other employers in northwest Ohio, southern Michigan, and Eastern Indiana. In 1984 I formed my own agency called Creative Insurance Resources, Inc. and focused purely on the group insurance marketplace. Since it was a very small agency, I relied on the resources of others to bring knowledge, expertise, and assorted services to my clients.

I recall at one point that the TPA I was working with was only quoting a few different reinsurance sources. These were their preferred markets and the relationships that they had, and they probably received commission overrides or some other incentive. At one point for a given case, I was asked, "How much do you want?" (Meaning, how much revenue did I want to make on this case?)

I said, "I don't know, what is the commission?"

The owner of the TPA said, "No, how much do you want?"

Again, I said, "I don't know. What is typically paid on this size of group with the commissions?"

He said, "How much do you want - $5 per employee per month, $20 per employee per month?" After doing the math, we agreed on a particular fee, but I didn't know at the time that the TPA was collecting all the commissions and that my compensation was over and above all the commissions.

I built a reasonable book of business in the group insurance market and in 1990 was approached by a Property-Casualty agency to help grow their benefits operation. I think I was the 65th or 66th employee of the agency, and they had three offices in the Midwest. When I resigned at the end of 2008, they had almost 700 employees in 12 offices. Needless to say, it was a very successful change in my career and successful endeavor for the agency.

IN 2008, I WAS RECRUITED BY A Wisconsin-based agency that wanted to open operations in Colorado. Because of my business history in Colorado and the fact that I had graduated from school there, it was a no-brainer for me. My wife and I eagerly jumped at the chance and I started working there on January 1, 2009 in the same capacity that I had with my prior agency — as a Client Executive.

This agency started an operation in Denver and was both a Property-Casualty and benefits shop. Unfortunately, after three years, they decided to pull out of Colorado due to the lack of new business revenue. This was primarily related to lack of production in Property-Casualty business, and the inability to obtain a relationship with a Workers' Compensation carrier in Colorado. They also failed to extend their existing relationships with Property-Casualty insurance companies from Wisconsin to Colorado. In other words, there were larger brokers in Colorado who already had relationships with the same insurance companies, and those insurance companies didn't want to disrupt those relationships by licensing another broker who would be deemed a competitor to the existing broker. When they pulled out, they told me that they wanted to keep me for an indefinite period of time, but that they would have problems servicing Colorado-based clients on the Western slope from Madison, Wisconsin.

After four months in that extended relationship, I was approached by another agency based in Denver that wanted to purchase my existing book of business and wanted me to become a producer for their agency. This was a different role for me: instead of being a Client Executive who is responsible for all aspects of each client— from initial marketing, selling, and onboarding a new client to the renewal of the client and everything in between, to one of a Producer—whereby I was solely responsible for new business production, and no subsequent responsibilities with the client (see Chapter 1).

Quite frankly, it was difficult to let go. From my prior experience as a Client Executive, I knew as much or more than the team I would turn those duties over to. When something associated with the group did or did not occur, I would get involved with the client, which the team didn't necessarily like. They would go to their supervisor and tell them that Frank was involved with the client. Their supervisor would then go to my supervisor, who would then take me to the woodshed and tell me to stop; that my responsibility was new business production, not consulting with the   client.

My tenure there lasted three years and my resignation stemmed from my frustration with their overall service levels, not following through with commitments, and an overall a lack-adaisical attitude of the team towards lowering my clients' costs. In most cases, once we would get a Broker of Record letter, we would continue servicing the current program that the previous broker had put in place with minor changes or improvements. What value did that bring?

I felt that my clients bought their programs from me; that they trusted me. And I felt responsible for helping them implement the programs that I brought to the table and that ultimately resulted in on-boarding them as a new client.

IN AUGUST OF 2015, I STARTED my own company, Strategic Healthplan Consulting LLC. My mission is to lower healthcare costs, challenge the status quo, and make a difference. Unlike the broker and agency models that I will describe later in this book, my approach is to work directly with my clients to move the needle: advise, educate, and coach them so that they can make informed decisions that will allow them to offer plans to their employees that are affordable, and plans that are financially sustainable for the future.

I wrote this book so that businesses can now understand what brokers do and don't do; what approaches they take and why; what motivates and drives them to do certain things, but ignore other opportunities for you. This book is about how you can become more informed about your broker, the agency you're dealing with, and what you can do to improve the financial performance of your plan.

This book is to show you that you don't know what you don't know — about your broker, about financial planning, about your insurance company. This book is written in two parts. The first 8 chapters will provide you with an understanding of what brokers and agencies do and don't do for their clients, what motivates them, tools that they may or may not have to help manage their client's plan, and what they should be doing to help lower costs for their clients in the most productive way.

The remaining chapters are a compilation of experiences

written to explain and demonstrate actual events and occurrences that I've encountered over 40 years in the industry with what employers, businesses, brokers, and other related parties have done to either miss opportunities for lowering their costs, or simply things that the employers or brokers haven't thought about or taken advantage of because ***THEY DON'T KNOW WHAT THEY DON'T KNOW.***

AGENCIES

INSURANCE AGENCIES CAN TAKE MANY forms and sizes: product lines, personnel, resources, departments, etc. All agencies provide some levels of these, according to my experience of owning an agency as well as the experiences of working for three others, and competing against other agencies over my 40-year career. Certainly there are variations between any of these depending on personnel, revenue, insurance market relationships, lines of coverage, and geographic footprint. For instance, small, independent agencies typically are associated with Property-Casualty products and programs. If they work in the group life and health arena, they typically only dabble in that line of coverage, so their real area of expertise does not lend itself well to their clients.

These agencies depend on the resources of the insurance companies they represent to provide many of the additional services and programs that larger agencies might otherwise provide on their own. It would not be unusual for one of their small business Property-Casualty clients to inquire at renewal whether or not their agency can provide them with alternative quotes for health insurance. The agency, in turn, might contact a few different group insurance representatives with health insurance companies and ask them for a quote, present it to the client, and, if it costs less than the incumbent, the client might purchase it from them. Other than the quoting process and renewal marketing, all services to the client come from the insurance company itself.

Small, independent agencies don't have the breadth and depth of resources to provide supplemental programs and services to their clients. They typically lack sophistication in the marketplace with respect to alternatively funded programs, and/or they are not well educated in those programs. If their clients have a number of questions about the overall program, or employees have numerous and frequent questions about how this plan works, or other difficult and significant issues, the small, independent agency doesn't have the manpower and/or man-hours to serve a larger client. Therefore, this type of agency generally approaches smaller and unsophisticated new prospects and clients that are in their comfort zone.

As you can imagine, an agency is built upon personal relationships that may go back years and years; they are not necessarily built on knowledge and expertise — or, should I say, the lack of knowledge and expertise. Again, a client doesn't know what they don't know. Usually, the only time that an agency is exposed with respect to service and/or issues is when there's a claim. So, in between the time of the sale and the point where a complicated claim comes up, you don't know what is going on in the agency, or what is not going on in the agency, or what the broker is doing, or is not doing, or should be doing.

I REMEMBER CALLING on a small municipality on the Western Slope of Colorado a few years ago. This group had purchased from—and serviced from—a small, local agency and had said that they were quite content. Being a municipality, they were always looking for a better deal, but at the same time, they were loyal to their broker, who they thought was doing a good job. Being new in Colorado at the time, I asked if they would like to see an alternative program, if it didn't take much of their time or effort in order to give me the information I needed to research the marketplace. They were happy to give me a shot. They gave me all the information I needed and I went out to market.

When I received back the first round of proposals, I found that none of them were competitive — at least competitive enough to warrant a change, since, after all, they were pretty happy with where they were. So I went back into the marketplace a second time and came up with an alternative.

When I went to make my presentation, I said to the employer, "You didn't tell me you were quoting this with five other brokers." She laughed and I laughed, but I asked her whether or not she'd seen any competitive quotes from any of them. She indicated she had received one, but it wasn't competitive, and she hadn't heard from the other four, so she assumed that they had nothing competitive. I agreed.

I then said, "You didn't tell me how much you are spending for your current program." She said it was approximately

$300,000. When I showed her my proposal, her eyes got   as big as saucers.

My quote for a better plan came in at $196,000. She then asked me why she had not seen a proposal of this type before, and I said to her, "With all due respect, what you get is only as good as your broker. If he's getting highly compensated by the insurance company from your current program, why would he show you anything else?"

The point of this is that while they were very happy where they were, and happy with their broker relationship, they had no idea that there were other programs out there that they should have been considering, and they didn't know why their current broker hadn't researched those alternative markets.

Just like the municipality that I encountered and their broker/agency relationship, small agencies must maximize revenue from whatever source they can. Insurance companies, while offering all the support to agencies regarding service, pay brokers handsomely through commissions. Brokers are nothing more than the distribution source for insurance companies. So when they distribute the insurance company's products, the insurance company pays them a handsome commission— similar to a tangible product that a sales rep would distribute.

When a broker hits a certain level of total overall premiums with a particular insurance company, the insurance company then begins to pay brokers an override. An override is additional commission compensation based upon that broker's book of business with that particular insurance company. In most cases, the commission override can exceed the sum of all commissions for that broker's book of business. It's understandable that when a broker is in their comfort zone with an insurance company and receives tremendous compensation from that insurance company, they won't go outside of their comfort zone or outside of their book of business to shop for more competitive, alternative programs for their clients.

One thing my father always told me when I got into the business was, "Always put your clients' needs ahead of your own and everything will take care of itself." In my opinion, small brokers and large brokers alike don't always heed that advice. When a broker is going to get paid less to distribute a different product— albeit a better product— they are more motivated to stay in their comfort zone and sell a product that pays more.

ANOTHER CONCERN WITH SMALL AGENCIES is that in many cases a client may not know what other services are available through other brokers. They think that all brokers are the same, and that they provide the same array of products and services — but that couldn't be farther from the truth. If a client or prospect is not exposed to other brokers, how are they to know what else is out there? Not just in terms of alternative products and health plans, but related services that some brokers can or cannot provide.

Larger, regional agencies similar to the ones that I worked for are also predominantly Property-Casualty revenue- driven agencies. The revenue associated with group health plans and group insurance plans in general isn't necessarily sufficient enough to stand on its own. Therefore, most of the resources, programs, and personnel are also devoted to the Property-Casualty lines of business. I'm sure there are exceptions to the rule, but health insurance brokers don't necessarily have the same level of knowledge, expertise, and sophistication that many of their counterparts who specialize in Property-Casualty programs (e.g., surety, environment, cyber risk, D&O, etc.) have.

One of the things I encountered in all three agencies I worked with was a lack of desire for a Property-Casualty Client Executive or Producer to introduce a Benefits person to their client. They were always worried that the Benefits person would screw things up and they might lose their Property-Casualty client altogether. My point was always that a) we wouldn't screw it up, but more importantly b) if you don't bring us in, your competition might bring in their Benefits person(s).

Large agencies have the ability to create new departments and new programs that smaller agencies cannot provide. This is mainly the result of revenue, which can be used to provide services better than those of the competition in their particular marketplace. Everyone has to be bigger and better than their competitors, so it's a definite problem if that agency doesn't utilize their resources to the fullest extent.

It's a waste of money to purchase programs if they can't provide agency expertise when they roll that program out. Or worse yet, they might promise to a prospective client that they're going to provide those services and resources, but ultimately do not utilize them. In other words, they may tell a prospective client all the good things they have done, and all the great things they can do, but don't implement the programs because either they may be too costly to operate on a month-to-month basis, or they don't have enough knowledge and expertise to carry them out efficiently and effectively.

THERE ARE TYPICALLY TWO MODELS that larger agencies utilize for their sales, service, and support personnel. The first type of agency — and the one that I was associated with throughout most of my career — was a three-tier approach. My title was an Account Executive, sometimes referred to as a Client Executive. I was responsible for new business production (i.e., selling and on-boarding a new client), all of the service during the course of the year, and conducting the entire renewal process. The buck stopped in my lap. I was responsible for everything associated with that client. I had Account Managers that helped me with day-to-day service for my clients, who helped clients with day-to-day claim issues, questions, employee meetings, and so on. In addition, there were other assorted support personnel that would assist with marketing, word processing, reporting, etc.

This model can be highly successful — until capacity is reached. The capacity of the Client Executive in the overall book of business that they're responsible for, as well as the capacity of the Account Managers, can't be spread too thin among a large variety of different clients. When this capacity is reached, the agency then has a choice: they can transfer accounts to a less experienced Account Executive or Client Executive and his or her team, or the agency can choose to have that Client Executive and the team stop selling and bringing in new business, and just continue to serve their book of business more effectively and efficiently.

Usually the agency takes the former position and therefore transfers clients to less experienced Account Executives who, again, may or may not be doing their due diligence at renewal (looking at alternative programs, for example) because of their inexperience and lack of knowledge.

The other type of agency is one that adds another layer to

the mix. I was a Producer in this model— also the one that I fit into most recently. In this role, I was solely responsible for bringing in new business. Once a new group came on board, I would turn it over to a service team, which was made up of an Account Executive, Account Manager, and the rest of the support team.

Once that group was on board, I would move onto the next prospect and the next opportunity. With respect to the new client that I had just brought to the agency, my role then changed to that of a Client Relationship Manager. In other words, instead of all of the ongoing service and communication with the client, I simply took them out to lunch on occasion and asked him, "How are we doing?" My service team took care of everything else.

When you have this particular model, there can be a very real disconnect between those who make the promises and those who keep the promises. It's very easy for everybody's agenda to get mixed up. When a client buys from me, trusts me, I feel responsible. And when the agenda of my team isn't the same as my or my client's expectations, trouble begins.

While this model may lend itself to higher and faster new business production and sales, the problem is that you have to have personnel that are compatible with the client and ones that communicate very frequently and carry out the promises of the Producer. Without lots of good communication, this model can result in very short-term relationships between the agency and the client.

A REQUEST FOR PROPOSAL (RFP) asks questions about an agency and/or agency resources. It's extremely important to know the structure of those you will be dealing with. If you end up having different relationships with the people you initially speak to, and those who make the sale and the presentation, chances are you may not receive the type of programs and services that were promised to you. Much like the Producer who brings on a new client and hands it off to a team of other individuals, in my opinion, it is better to work with the entire team from the get-go.

When interviewing agencies for your business, you will want to actually have not only the biographies and resumes of the people you're working with, but also face-to-face interviews with the prospective team so that you know of or can anticipate any personality conflicts. At that time, you can also talk about your agenda and the timeline in which you have to implement the programs and services.

I'm not a big fan of RFPs because the responses may falsely illustrate the real inner workings of the agency. It's easy for an agency to embellish beyond reality programs that they presumably offer. They can talk about how good they are in the programs they offer, but in reality it's "what have you actually done for other clients? Give me references and case studies of what you've done with the programs and resources that you have said you have and that you've identified— resources that can make a difference between you and your competitors." As an employer, you don't want ideologies, concepts, and theories that have no application to your situation, your employees, and your environment and culture.

All agencies can brag about how much better they are than their competitors. While everyone talks the talk, very few can actually walk the walk. In any given subject in an RFP, or response to a question in an RFP, I would ask not only for the response to the question, but also examples, references, and case studies that you can actually follow up on. Too many times I walked into a prospective client's office only to hear that their broker said they would do one thing but never did.

Agencies may tell you about all the products and services they offer, all the markets that they can cover, all the data analytics that they have, and everything else under the sun but buyer beware: you may not get what you think you're getting get at the end of the day. What can this agency bring to the table that can actually lower the cost of healthcare — not the price of my premiums or my administrative fees? What are they going to do to actually lower the cost?

WHEN IT COMES TO DEPARTMENTS AND PERSONNEL, agencies have different approaches and styles of management. The segregation of duties is the most appropriate and productive way to get the most out of your agency. When you have an individual doing multiple tasks for numerous clients, duties and projects are prioritized and not necessarily on a timeline that is suitable for you.

For example, in the Benefits department, where I started in my first agency job, we had a separation of duties whereby as a Client Executive I was responsible for overseeing all of the duties that the various personnel performed for my clients. While I had Account Managers performing day-to-day service duties, there were other individuals responsible for all of the marketing of renewals and new business opportunities, also different individuals responsible for conducting all the reporting, other personnel responsible for wellness and disease management, a department for word processing and spreadsheets, and I was fortunate enough to also have an assistant Client Executive to help manage these individuals for my entire book of business.

In my role as a Producer, there were three people who essentially did all the duties and everyone was working at capacity. So the Account Executive was doing strategic oversight over the other two people— the Account Manager dealing with day-to-day issues, and an Account Analyst doing all the reporting for all of their clients. It can be overwhelming as people are overworked, and projects tend to get delayed or not completed in a timely manner.

These are questions that most clients have not asked their broker, and even if they did, they didn't go into enough depth and detail to really know how they would be serviced and what's going to happen in the future.

BROKER AND AGENCY KNOWLEDGE

AS ONE WOULD EXPECT, the personnel at an agency need to have a great deal of knowledge, expertise, experience, and sophistication when it comes to group health plans. It's a mistake to think that an agency can hire someone in a different field and instantly make them an insurance professional at an agency where a high level of service knowledge is required.

All insurance agents and brokers who want to do business in a particular state must complete a 40-hour course, and must pass an exam, after which they can become licensed in that state — another requirement. They must also meet other personal criteria such as a credit check and motor vehicle check. Simply passing the exam doesn't make one an expert, nor does the exam cover enough information about group health to give an individual the ability to serve their clients at a high level.

In most states the actual material that you study, including the life and health licensing exam, is really more oriented towards life insurance and annuities rather than health insurance. There really isn't any licensing information in the material other than individual accident and health, and there's no information about pharmacy benefit managers, self- funding, alternatively funded programs, etc. This particular knowledge and experience is gathered either by attending seminars or training within the agency, or trial by fire. Most commonly, it's trial by fire. As a neophyte salesperson in the insurance business, or a neophyte in health insurance, sometimes the best method to learn is to shadow another more experienced Account Manager or Account Executive to gain more knowledge.

As you can imagine, a lot of the information about group health insurance, Affordable Care Act (ACA) compliance, and all the other aspects of employee benefit programs are acquired through self-teaching or through the experience of another member of the team. While there is material available in the market through subscriptions and other manuals, these are typically not a source of information for a new Agent or Producer working with an agency. Seminars can be held by insurance companies, but the subject matter is usually strictly related to their specific products and programs. Therefore, it's difficult to gain a thorough understanding of programs that compete against each other when trying to investigate all of the concerns that a prospective employer has. It's too easy to show all the basic information to an employer but not go into detail. This is where trouble arises.

The same holds true when working with alternatively funded programs. These could include programs such as retrospective premium, a minimum premium program, partial self-funding, ASO, or the discussion and merits of bundled versus unbundled plans.

There are so many nuances and practices that insurance companies follow with their respective programs— you cannot assume that all companies follow the same practices. Everyone is different. And, in order to offer these programs to clients within a respective state, they all need to be licensed with the Department of Insurance— hence also the disparity between programs.

It's important to note that many insurance companies and claims administrators tout their ability to process claims very quickly. While you may think this is critical and impressive, it can also be very misleading. The reason they make the statement about fast processing is that the vast majority of claims are auto-adjudicated where no human being reviews them for accuracy or appropriateness. Their plan of benefits for their clients is designed to coincide with their hardware and software systems that permit this very quick adjudication of the claim. What you lose is the ability to customize a plan for the client so that it's a plan that the employer wants to buy and offer their employees, rather than a plan that the insurance company wants to sell to the employer. When a plan is template driven, it may provide for faster adjudication, but customization is sacrificed. Everything must fit into their mold.

BUNDLED VS. UNBUNDLED

WHEN IT COMES TO PARTIAL SELF-FUNDING, there are two categorical opportunities that exist. The first is what can be referred to as a bundled plan. A bundled plan is one that has all aspects of a self-funded program under one umbrella — the insurance company. This includes administration, stop-loss insurance, Pharmacy Benefit Management (PBM), networks, plan design — everything that goes into the Benefits program for the employer and their employees.

The advantage of this is that it's all under one roof. The disadvantage of it is that you lose all customization utilizing independent, Best-in-Class vendors. In summary, everything is owned and/or controlled by the insurance company itself and the employer must work within the plan for what they deem to be appropriate for their group. Because the selection is limited, so is the competitiveness. In other words, if you can't pick and choose from different independent companies and vendors— you only can pick ones that are offered by that insurance company— you must take that price with very little or no negotiation. One size fits all. One price fits all.

By contrast, an unbundled plan is one that utilizes independent vendors to provide all of the same programs and services that the insurance company provides. These include an independent Third Party Administrator (TPA), stop-loss reinsurance, PBM, customized plan design, PPO networks, etc. The advantage of this is that each of these programs can be shopped, investigated, and researched (presumably by the broker) to select the most appropriate vendor for their prospective client. Normally this is done through a Request For Proposal (RFP) process. Obviously, the important thing would be to know whether the appropriate questions are being asked in the RFP, or if it's more related to basic information and of course, price.

There are countless situations that I've encountered with agencies that request information in an RFP about a particular vendor. More often than not, basic questions— fundamental questions— are asked within the RFP rather than getting to the real, relevant topics and details that differentiate one vendor from another. Again, most questions only scratch the surface and once you get past the basic, fundamental information about that vendor, it always seems to come back to price. The problem is that brokers don't understand enough about these independent vendors to ask the appropriate and relevant questions; and therefore, decisions are ultimately made based on price (since the employer thinks that they're all the same). In the end, it's not about price— it's about capabilities. When examining vendors, you need to know what their abilities and capabilities are.

Price can be negotiated; capabilities cannot. Because most brokers don't take the time to understand how these vendors operate, they obviously cannot ask the relevant questions that need to be understood and presented to their clients.

In many cases, the selection of vendors by a broker for their client— whether bundled or unbundled— is motivated by the broker's compensation. If a broker gets paid more by one insurance company than by another, they are often more likely to present that to their clients, assuming that the recommended vendor can more or less provide the same service. **You don't know what you don't know** — the employer never knows what is out there and what is possible because the broker hasn't done their research or doesn't understand who the really good players in the marketplace are and who is just average. And just like any product or service, there are those who are excellent, average, and below average.

A broker's motivation to make a particular recommendation may also include their relationship with that particular insurance company or vendor. It may have more to do with that relationship than what the provider can actually do for the client and their employees. There may be undisclosed compensation, vacation trips, or other tangible rewards for placing an insurance contract and building a book with that particular insurance company, which in turn leads to more and more recommendations of that company by that broker. You'd be surprised how often brokers make recommendations based on relationships rather than in-depth analyses and scrutiny of the insurance company or vendor's ability to provide the best service and meet the specific needs of the client.

Another item to consider is the ability or inability of the insurance company or the administrator to deviate from their practices to accommodate not just plan customization, but the utilization of other assorted vendors. For example, will an insurance company permit the use of a stop-loss carrier other than the one that they own? Will they permit a different PBM other than what they own in order to lower the cost of prescriptions for employees? Do they have the ability to interface with vendors such as small regional PPO networks, or vendors who re-price claims based upon Reference-Based Pricing (RBP)? Can they accommodate a Resource-Based Relative Value System

(RBRVS) for physician pricing?

Chances are an insurance company will not permit this—they want to use their own programs and products so that they, in turn, can make more money and be more profitable. In an unbundled situation, the TPA may have its own favorite stop-loss markets, or a particular PBM that they want to use, and will not permit customization and integration for their clients with something other than what they control and make a profit from. Other TPAs may offer integration with other selected vendors.

ERISA requires complete transparency, although you will find that this is not the case in real practice. Insurance companies and administrators don't necessarily disclose all compensation that they pay. The insurance broker doesn't necessarily disclose all the compensation they receive, either. There may be backdoor deals, hidden fees, and charges that the employer bears and the broker realizes. In many cases, a broker doesn't want to disclose how much they're earning because it may come under the scrutiny of the employer. The employer should attempt to lower their costs and compensation to their broker if the broker is only marketing insurance and/or with other vendors. They should get paid for that service. It doesn't take a lot of man-hours to find the best program for their client, particularly if they do this on a regular basis.

I can recall on more than one occasion when I was putting together a program for a client and the agency wanted to use a particular PBM. This PBM was not a bad PBM, but it wasn't quite as good as others. However, it paid the agency a handsome sum of money— derived from per- prescription fees and rebates — over the course of the year. Having actually sat across the table from the PBM, the PBM asked me about the rebate, "How much would you like? Do you want 15¢ on the dollar, 25¢ on the dollar? Do you want a fee of $1 per prescription too?" These are all unnecessary fees that employers unknowingly pay to their broker, and the broker may not disclose them. It simply raises the cost of healthcare for their employees.

Insurance brokers are notorious for performing a lot of marketing and perhaps helping with a few claim issues during the course of the year, and then showing up at the end of the year with a renewal — typically an increase. They may also show up with an alternative to either justify the increase or in some cases, legitimately suggest an option. When considering an option that requires a change of players or change of vendors, it's important to know that those rates are typically quoted on an immature basis, e.g., 9 months of claims versus 12 months of claims due to claims lag.

Claims lag is a phenomenon that occurs when an employee incurs a claim on one date and the claim is paid 60 to 90 days later. As a result, at the end of the year, the employer has really only encountered 9 to 10 months of actual claim payments. The insurance company knows this and will lower their premiums in the first year to appear attractive only to raise the rates significantly in the second year. If you have 9 months' worth of claims in a 12-month period, and you need to increase this to 12 months' worth of claims in a 12-month period, then that's a 33% increase. Favorable claims experience in the first 9 months may lower the premiums, but nonetheless, the increase is inevitable.

As a result of the small amount of effort required to perform the marketing functions above, it should be noted that the compensation to the broker should be commensurate with that service. The problem is that a large agency requires the revenue to run their entire operation, building, and everything in it: overhead, utilities, salaries, and, benefits — everything associated with any other business— so they try to *maximize* the revenue stream from their clients. **You don't know what you don't know** — what the appropriate compensation structure is for the actual services performed. Rather, the broker gets paid the commissions offered by the insurance company to distribute their product. This is built into your premium along with any other overrides associated with the book of business.

WE'VE ALREADY DISCUSSED HOW brokers tend to rely on insurance companies for the services that they offer to their clients. It's not uncommon for a broker to make a recommendation of an insurance company and have the employer sign all the contracts, only to discover at termination, for example, that there are consequences for termination— even more so for early termination.

In an unbundled program, this is the case even more often. Since the broker has not done their due diligence and an in-depth review of a TPA and their TPA contracts and services, they may not know how that TPA operates; they may not know their processes and reporting capabilities; and they may not know their contracts either (termination), so they rely on the TPA even more. If the broker is relying on the TPA to provide other vendors such as the PBM, stop- loss, etc., they are really setting themselves up for heavy reliance on that TPA. Again, this is because they haven't done enough research and due diligence on the vendors that the TPA puts in place.

It's extremely important that you, as a client, know more than you care to know about your broker— what they know and what they don't know, how they get paid, what the relationship is with the vendors— you want full transparency and disclosure, *everything* about that broker. All brokers are not the same, nor are the services that they perform.

SELLING

GENERALLY SPEAKING, THERE ARE TWO basic approaches to acquiring new business: 1) quoting alternative plans that compete favorably with the incumbent program and broker, and 2) acquiring the business on a broker of record letter (BOR) or agent of record letter (AOR). In some cases it's not uncommon that a broker uses both depending on the lines of business.

I recall from working for my old agency back in the Midwest that their typical mode of operation was to quote and compete. Our approach was to get an opportunity to quote at the renewal or anniversary date of the prospect. This usually took place several months in advance so that all decisions could be made and implementation could occur on a timely basis — that way, there was no interruption for the employees.

We would essentially tell the prospect how good our agency was and that we had a history of providing very competitive quotes and would like to have an opportunity to show them what we are capable of. We would then go out to market and see if we could beat other agencies' current prices. The initial attention was given to price, not the plan of benefits or any other consideration if we couldn't beat it. If we couldn't beat the price, then we would typically walk away.

The problem with this approach is that it was all about price, not value. Further, it neglected to initially take into consideration their exact level of benefits. Therefore, it is not uncommon to return with a slightly different set of benefits, or significantly different benefits, or a different network — or some rather significant variation of what they currently had.

Our quotes would end up on a spreadsheet and we would take that into the prospect and hopefully the difference was compelling enough that they would either overlook the differences in plans, or that the prospect would decide the differences weren't significant enough.

We would always go to our preferred markets, where we not only got a quick turnaround of the quotes, but ultimately received more favorable compensation from them. We were comfortable with the service that we received and the responsiveness that we would get. We had a requirement that the company we were using had to have a rating of A- or better for us to consider them. We didn't want our client to get into a situation where the company defaulted — that would create havoc with employees. Any carrier that has less than an A- rating is susceptible to that. If I had a carrier that the agency was unfamiliar with, I would be discouraged from going to that carrier (not forbidden, but discouraged) because the compensation might not be as high. However, with new carriers getting into the marketplace at that time and other carriers leaving the marketplace, there were a lot of revolving doors and associated people within the industry that changed from one carrier to another.

Depending on the size of the prospect, i.e., the number of employees they had and the type of funding arrangement we were pursuing, in most cases we wrote an RFP for the carriers, requesting what we wanted to have them illustrate. We would include claims data and other relevant information. This, in turn, would produce a response to the RFP and a proposal by the insurance company. The problem was that our RFP was so basic that we didn't really understand how those companies operated, what their practices were, or anything about their contracts.

Depending on why you decide to change brokers, it's important to have the prospective brokers disclose everything about themselves and their agency. In addition, you need to ask them the question: what are you going to do with the current program to make it better? What are you going to do that our current broker hasn't done or can't do? Again, buyer beware: you may be told a story or given promises that cannot be kept.

In a previous chapter, I talked about an experience I had with an employer who said to me, "Why haven't I seen this before?" I indicated to her at that time that due to the nature of brokers and their compensation of commissions and overrides, that the quote was only as good as what her broker wanted to show her, meaning that brokers may choose not to show certain carriers because they don't get compensated enough.

It's very important to know what markets your brokers are going to and what sort of relationship they have with those particular markets. There's nothing wrong with going to a limited number of markets; it's just that you may not see the entire marketplace, and as a result, you may not be shown the best or most competitive program.

INSURANCE CARRIERS AND OTHER VENDORS typically have two types of policies when it comes to broker requests. One company may give proposals out to every broker who requests them, while another insurance company might only give out a proposal to the first broker who requests one. The problem with the latter is that a broker may request a quote from an insurance company and has no intention of showing it to you. Since that broker might be the first one requesting the quote, they have blocked all other brokers from the ability to get one as well. The important thing to understand here is that the insurance company that's being blocked may be the most competitive one, but may not pay the highest commission. Therefore, you have no knowledge of their quote if they're blocked.

The method of providing everybody with a quote can be equally damaging. I know of numerous situations and cases where a broker has submitted incomplete data and/or hidden information that might tend to otherwise generate a higher premium, so they've effectively been issued a quote by the insurer based on incomplete or false information. The broker wants their quote to be the most competitive so they get the business.

Another broker would then come in with more complete data and hope that they would get a competitive quote as well. Then, I would come in with complete and thorough data (even if it's bad news), but providing it would give the underwriter the most accurate picture of what's really going on with the group. At this point, the underwriter would be totally confused because they've received inconsistent data from all of us, and would then have a tendency to either a) not give out any quotes or b) err on the side of caution and give out a very high or conservative quote. The first two brokers had polluted the marketplace by not providing thorough and complete data that reflects the actual claims experience of the group. This is obviously a problem!

This can also occur at renewal with your current plan when your current broker, while shopping the marketplace, doesn't disclose everything that needs to be disclosed. He or she comes back to you with a renewal response from the incumbent carrier (therefore keeping your plan with the same carrier and perhaps a high renewal increase and higher commissions), or they come back to you with extremely competitive rates — however once that plan is selected, you find that the carrier will then refuse to honor those initial rates until all required information is provided and disclosed.

You don't know what you don't know. You don't know whether your broker is acting in the best interest of you the client, or themselves the broker. You don't know whether they've attempted to block other broker competitors, or whether they're going to show you all the quotes that they've obtained. You don't know whether they've disclosed everything that needs to be disclosed to provide you with a realistic and accurate proposal, or whether they're trying to shortcut the arrangement just to get a lower quoted price.

I realize you have to trust someone, but on many occasions I've seen that trust be exploited to the point where it's the client who's on the receiving end of bad news, higher prices, and inaccurate or incomplete quotes.

The same holds true with quoting vendors in an unbundled situation. Those vendors will have the same set of rules that insurance companies do, and will either honor first-come, first-serve, or provide a quote based upon the information received. In many cases, when they provide quotes based on the information they receive, there is a checklist of outstanding information that they require before those quotes are firm. Therefore, the quotes are conditional. They don't know who has control with the client and the best relationship with the client; therefore, they may give out quotes to everyone with the hope and expectation that they get the business regardless of the broker.

WHEN IT COMES TO THE unbundled program, one of the most important financial elements is the stop-loss reinsurance. There are many, many reinsurance companies in the marketplace and Managing General Underwriters (MGU) that offer stop-loss coverage. Most TPAs will shop stop-loss upon request, but they typically utilize only a handful of select carriers that they have relationships with. Larger agencies will also have relationships with their carriers, but again, they may be few in number and may not include MGUs. Smaller agencies are going to rely on the TPA to do the stop-loss marketing because they have no relationship with anyone. It's very important that you "cover the waterfront" with respect to getting realistic quotes from the various stop-loss markets. And it's important that the carriers that have been illustrated to you are A- rated or better.

I can't tell you the number of times that I've gone into a competitive environment and the employer has told me that they can't get a stop-loss quote or a competitive stop- loss quote because nobody "wants them". There is a price for everything. It's more likely that the broker was unable to find something for their client because they had very limited access to or knowledge of the marketplace.

The same thing holds true with Pharmacy Benefit Managers (PBM). This is an extremely important element in an unbundled, self-funded plan because of the rapidly increasing costs of prescription drugs. It's very important to have quotes from the most competitive PBMs in the market, and the quoting process can be very confusing and difficult for a broker who is unsophisticated and/or has little to no knowledge of what constitutes one competitive PBM from another. The reality is that there is a stark and clear difference between PBMs, the costs of their drugs, their fees, and their rebates. It takes a broker who has a complete and thorough understanding of how a PBM works and the components that go into competitiveness, in order to get the most competitive program for your employees at the lowest price.

With partial self-funding becoming more popular in the marketplace due to the ACA, many brokers have a higher comfort level with insurance companies that offer their version of self-funded plans or something that is referred to as an ASO — Administrative Services Only. These are bundled, self-funded plans underwritten by the insurance company. Brokers have a higher comfort level because more of the work in building and servicing the program is under the umbrella of the insurance company, unlike an unbundled plan. Since the insurance company puts everything together in the bundled plan, it's a one-stop shop for brokers who don't have as much knowledge of the component parts. It's easier for them to call up their insurance representative when there's a problem and have them do the legwork.

There is also another variety of alternatively funded arrangements that have been historically available in the marketplace, or have recently been designed by insurance companies to attract smaller, partially self-funded prospects. These programs may look, smell, taste, and feel like a fully insured plan, and they may be considered in some states as fully insured, but they are a version of a bundled, partially self- funded plan. They have many attractive features; however, they are bundled, and options within the plan are few. Still, I've had clients who have enrolled in these plans and have done very well financially with them.

All plans are only as good as the broker. If the broker has no knowledge of these programs, their client will never see them. The programs will never be given the light of day. If a broker historically has a comfort level with an insurance company, then that's where they will go to look for alternatively funded programs. If that company doesn't have any, then they will come back to you, the client, with nothing.

You don't know what you don't know. You don't know what sort of relationships brokers have with carriers, what their knowledge level is, what their expertise is, or what kind of access they have to the marketplace. You don't know their knowledge level of specific programs within your unbundled package, how contracts work and the like.

COMPENSATION

BROKER COMPENSATION CAN COME in a variety of ways — some are disclosed and some are not. Usually, compensation comes in the form of commissions and/or fees that are charged to you, the client. You may think that the insurance company or some other vendor is paying the brokers, but you are mistaken. The commissions and/or fees may be paid by the insurance company or vendor, but they are added to your premiums or service fees.

Usually, the broker decides the amount of commissions. When quoting a particular fully insured plan, a broker may request a 5% commission built into the premium. This would be across all lines of coverage (medical and Rx) and would be paid by the insurance company to the broker as you pay your monthly premium.

While disclosure is required under ERISA for groups over 100 lives, not all compensation is necessarily disclosed. On products like stop-loss, the commission could be up to 15% of the premium. The broker could choose to receive less than 15%, and they sometimes do, but the broker may not be disclosing the actual percentage. Commissions should be disclosed on Form 5500 on an annual basis, and the insurance company or Third Party Administrator usually files this on behalf of the employer. Those commissions aren't always accurate and may not include all lines of coverage, depending on the size of the group.

Compensation can also be paid in a variety of fees. For an unbundled, self-funded health plan, fees generally are disclosed separately and then added back in as a line item to the TPA monthly invoice. However, some TPAs simply add the broker fees into their administration fees and may not disclose them separately. It simply increases the monthly administration charge to you, the client. In some cases the broker could be receiving both the commission on stop-loss and a fee on the administration. It's important to understand how much you're paying your broker and for what services.

All brokers are trying to maximize revenue because the

agency is attempting to cover all overhead and make a profit, and they ask their brokers to push the envelope and charge as much as possible until challenged or questioned by the client. After all, the broker shares in this revenue as well.

When evaluating a prospective client's benefit plan, I always look to understand and evaluate the amount of compensation that a broker is receiving. You would be shocked at the amount of revenue that is paid in any given group to a broker — in many cases, it is excessive in relation to the actual services being rendered. This is why brokers don't want to disclose their compensation for fear of having it either reduced or challenged by the employer, or they fear the employer will subsequently look for a different broker who charges less.

Brokers can also receive commissions on what's referred to as ancillary coverage. Ancillary lines of coverage would include dental, life insurance, AD&D, disability, vision, and the whole variety of supplemental products that are paid for by an employee — voluntary products. These commissions may not be disclosed either, but continue to add up for the broker's annual compensation. It's unfortunate that brokers tend to push the envelope for more and more revenue when the services they perform aren't necessarily commensurate with their compensation.

Another source of revenue that is often not disclosed — and is often abused — is a fee added on to the Pharmacy Benefit Manager (PBM) and prescription drugs. More often than not, the PBM will ask a broker how much they want to receive in the way of fees. They will tend to offer a fee per prescription and/or a percentage of the rebate. You would be hard pressed to know what those fees are when you sign your contract and/or even ask the broker for disclosure. The amount of fees paid in the Pharmacy space and the ones that are paid to the broker can be excessive, and this further adds to the lack of transparency and exorbitant costs that an employer pays for broker services.

In addition to the fees and commissions paid to a broker in a given case, insurance companies and stop-loss carriers also pay overrides onthebroker's entire book of business. Insurance companies will incentivize brokers to build their book with them through these overrides. Once a book of business (measured in premium) exceeds a certain threshold — for instance, $1 million — then the insurance company will pay an additional commission on that book of business. Each time an additional threshold is reached, a higher commission level is obtained. These, too, are ultimately built in the overall premiums for that broker's book of business and their clients' premiums. These are not additional expenses associated with the insurance company — everything is ultimately a pass- through to the employer.

When a broker has the opportunity to quote a case, they will tell the insurance company what commission rate they want built into the premium. Hopefully, it's low enough to make the premiums to the employer competitive. In some states, the amount of the commissions or fees is regulated for groups of less than 100 lives. With groups over 100 lives, the commission rates can be whatever the broker chooses. One can expect that if the premiums come in low and premium rates are competitive with the incumbent insurance carrier, then the broker may ask for higher commissions so that their rates are still competitive, but the broker receives additional compensation.

By contrast, when a broker receives an Agent of Record (AOR) or Broker of Record (BOR) letter on a given case, they will receive the same compensation that the previous broker had built in until the next renewal date and then everything is up for grabs again — the broker can ask for whatever commission they want. The same holds true with all renewal business, in that the commission rate can be different from year to year, which can also cause the premiums to go up or down.

THE PROBLEM WITH COMMISSIONS is that they artificially inflate the premium paid by the employer. They also provide the broker with an increase in revenue every year so that the employer gets a premium increase. The broker may or may not have done anything to deserve an increase in revenue, but it's automatically built in as an increase in revenue every single year because premiums are going up. One would think that the commission levels would go down commensurate with the increase in premium, but that's not the case unless specifically requested by the broker.

I recently met with a group that received a 23% increase from their insurance company at their renewal. While certainly unhappy with the increase, they didn't realize that their broker also received a 23% increase. When I asked the group what the broker had done during the year to earn a 23% increase in their revenue, I got blank stares and shrugged shoulders from them.

As I said earlier, brokers and agencies want to increase revenue so that overhead can be covered and profit margins can be maximized. Premiums are artificially increased when commissions are included. This is because when the commissions are added, they are also added to state premium taxes, underwriting fees, underwriting margins, etc., and increase the entire premium. These are not à la carte, fixed expenses — they are included and go up as the premium goes up, and when the premium includes commission, everything is increased.

Brokers can also receive additional compensation and profit-sharing bonuses based upon the profitability of their book of business. The insurance company looks at the profitability of the book of business — i.e., premiums versus claims — it equates to a loss ratio, and when the loss ratio is at or below an acceptable and agreed-upon threshold, the insurer will share some of their company surplus with the broker. While this is additional revenue to the broker and the agency, it is applied to the loss ratio of the book of business, as well as the respective groups that comprise the book.

Most employers have no idea how much the broker is making at their expense and from what sources. They typically don't ask the broker for disclosure and the broker doesn't offer it up. Unlike any other professional service such as attorney fees or accounting fees, one would always like to know what the hourly rate is. Insurance brokers don't necessarily follow rules of transparency and disclosure, and hidden revenue is their moniker.

There are methods to flush out all fees and commissions through disclosure and transparency so that an employer sufficiently and accurately knows what's being paid for the services that are being rendered. I'm of the opinion that brokers are overpaid for their services, as most brokers typically are involved in marketing and some day-to-day troubleshooting. They may do a little bit more work at renewal to try to drive the premiums down, but more often than not, the recommended change of insurance carriers notwithstanding, brokers typically recommend cost shifting to employees to mitigate premium increases — i.e. higher deductibles, co-pays, and out-of-pocket or employee contributions. **You don't know what you don't know.** A broker's compensation definitely increases your cost of doing business and the cost of your health insurance program.

I've had situations where my boss at the agency has told me to increase the fees on my self-funded clients so the fee would fit into their hierarchy of group revenue bracketing. In other words, groups under 100 lives had to have a certain minimum level of revenue; groups between 100 and 250 lives had to have a minimum of additional revenue; groups 250 to 500 had to have certain level of revenue, and so on. This wasn't based upon the actual services we offered, but rather the selected bracketing the agency wanted to charge for every group. Some groups received more services, and others got less, but it wasn't a case-by-case basis.

Other times, one of my clients would receive a massive increase in the premium, and the additional revenue generated to the agency was significant. I actually lowered the commission rate so that it lowered the increase in premiums, and our revenue remained flat. This did not sit well with the agency, because again, they're trying to maximize the revenue. And since it hadn't been disclosed, the client didn't know any different.

Sometimes, the commissions have well exceeded six figures on a medium-size group of less than 500 employees. This occurred to me when I took over a case on a BOR from a large national broker who was charging an exorbitant fee, and we were the beneficiaries of that large fee when we became the new Broker of Record.

I've had other situations where the commission wasn't enough in an unbundled, self-funded health plan, so we added a rather significant per-employee, per-month fee on top of the commission to reach those bracketing plateaus. There've also been cases where we eliminated commissions altogether and just charged a flat per-employee, per-month fee. However, it's a little embarrassing when a broker fee actually exceeds the fee of the Third Party Claims Administrator.

There are all kinds of games that are played with a broker's compensation. Can you imagine that it's all built in to the total administrative fee and not disclosed to the client? **You don't know what you don't know.**

MARKETING

THE MARKETING OF INSURANCE can be very fundamental and tricky at the same time. Marketing is a process whereby brokers perform a search and evaluation to try to find presumably lower-cost and more competitive programs for their clients. Of course, that process is only as good as the relationships that brokers have with various companies and the identification of the most appropriate and competitive insurance companies that they have access to. You're only as good as who you know. Insurance companies do a pretty good job of identifying consistent producers to educate them about their programs.

Brokers and agencies have a tendency to gravitate towards insurance companies and insurance representatives that they know and trust, and have continual exposure to. Understandably, brokers also gravitate towards those insurance companies that pay a higher commission.

Insurance agencies also have relationships with carriers that provide them with incentive income that's over and above the standard commissions paid to the agency or broker. These arrangements usually come as a result of the production of a book of business that is consistent and growing. A relationship with brokers who place one or two accounts a year with a carrier is not the kind of relationship that insurance companies necessarily care to have.

Typically, smaller agencies tend to have a smaller cadre of insurance companies for any given product line. In other words, they may go to a few carriers that call on them on a regular basis, and these carriers are not necessarily the same ones that larger agencies tend to go to. Larger agencies tend to have what they call their "preferred carriers", which provide higher compensation levels to those brokers who have larger books of business. Larger agencies may also utilize a greater number of carriers due to multiple and diverse product lines.

The question for employers is whether they're really getting a true and accurate look at the marketplace. Who are the carriers that my broker went to? Who are the ones that they chose *not* to approach? Are they approaching carriers only to block them from their competitors? Am I getting the best rate from that carrier, or might another broker otherwise improve upon it? How much compensation has the broker loaded in my rate? What are the financial ratings of the insurance companies? What references does the broker have for these companies?

Larger agencies may encourage their personnel to only market to their preferred carriers. This is true for life insurance, disability insurance, medical insurance, stop-loss, etc.

With the ancillary lines of coverage — i.e., life insurance, AD&D, disability insurance, etc. — most insurance companies will be fairly similar in their rates, while there may be differences in their respective benefits. When it comes to stop-loss insurance or other group health plans, there is a great deal of inconsistency. That's why it's important to have an expanded view of the marketplace to ensure that you're getting the most competitive rate. Let's break down each of these lines of coverage to better understand what's going on.

REQUESTING QUOTES

FIRST OF ALL, IT'S IMPORTANT to understand the actual process of marketing. This typically begins with the gathering of all the appropriate and accurate information. This includes a census that includes employee demographics, a description of plan design — which might be the current plan benefits summary or a Summary Plan Description (SPD) — all claims experience (when it can be obtained), rate history, and any other appropriate history/future plan descriptions.

Further, understand that not all brokers are necessarily knowledgeable about what to provide; therefore, there may be significant inconsistencies regarding what an underwriter might receive from multiple brokers. Some brokers intentionally eliminate certain types of claims experience because they think that it might be detrimental to them getting a competitive rate. Other brokers might send partial information, while others send all the necessary data information. The competition for new clients among brokers is fierce, and everyone tries to gain an edge.

Unfortunately, it's the client who's the recipient of this competition, and as a result, the client may receive rates that aren't as competitive as they might otherwise be. Also, when you have multiple brokers submitting Requests for Proposals (RFPs) to carriers, the result will only be as good as the information submitted. When receiving inconsistent   or incomplete data from multiple brokers, underwriters may refuse to offer a competitive quote at all because they don't know which broker's information to trust.

UNDERWRITERS

INSURANCE COMPANIES TYPICALLY HAVE TWO types of business practices when it comes to releasing quotes. The first is a first-come, first-serve policy in which only one broker gets a proposal, and the second is where they release a quote to anybody and everybody based upon the information received. Thus, we end up with quoting inconsistencies.

In some cases, and on a first-come, first-serve basis, the incumbent broker may go to a wide variety of insurance companies and may attempt to "block" their competition with no intention of ever showing that particular quote to their client, trying to lock up that particular market.

While this sounds unfair and probably is, it's a matter of an insurance company's practice when they only release one quote. Sometimes if the insurance company finds that the that the broker has consistently tried to block other brokers and has never presented their insurance company proposal, the insurance company might not offer any more quotes in the future — or the company may exclude that broker from their program altogether.

LIFE INSURANCE

ASSUMING THAT BROKERS ARE SUBMITTING the same thorough and accurate data, the amounts of coverage can sometimes vary, and thus so will the rates that a broker receives. For group life insurance, companies use a Commissioner's Standard Ordinary table to determine base rates using national mortality data.

There is also an element of their own company's claims experience for their entire book of business. Other factors such as industry age, gender, and location can also cause the base rate to vary. One would expect that most carriers have similar life insurance rates — and they do. Assuming all other things are equal, the variation in rates occurs in the contracts, benefits, commissions, fees, and underwriter surplus.

Underwriting surplus is a fund that underwriters can allocate towards the acquisition of new business and make themselves more competitive than their competitors. When their proposed rate might be very close to another insurance company's rate for group life insurance, an underwriter can use surplus to lower the overall annual premium by that amount. This makes the rate much more competitive initially, but at the end of the day, it's about loss ratio — the premium collected versus claims incurred. If after two or three years a loss ratio is unacceptable, the insurance carrier will raise the rate dramatically. The surplus didn't help the overall claims experience — it just lowered the initial price.

DISABILITY

WITH BOTH SHORT-TERM AND LONG-TERM disability, it's a relatively similar process to group life insurance. The insurance companies take all the relevant data to establish a base rate, and determine an annual premium based upon their claims experience and their book of business. They, too, can utilize surplus to lower the premium, which will ultimately affect the loss ratio.

Differences between insurance carriers and their contracts will also alter the rates. These differences include the definition of disability, the own occupation period, specialty definitions, elimination period, benefit period, partial disability benefit, residual disability definitions, and other bells and whistles that LTD carriers offer. It is extremely important to understand all these definitions, as they not only affect the benefit outcomes for the claimant, but also affect your price and premium.

DENTAL AND VISION

OTHER ANCILLARY PROGRAMS such as dental and vision are also rated the same way. These premiums are not of any significance compared to other programs, but there are differences in benefits and coverage, which could also affect the overall premium.

GROUP HEALTH INSURANCE

GROUP HEALTH INSURANCE IS ANOTHER story. Variations of fully insured plans and partially self-funded plans, in reality, are rated the same way. There are different components to each, but nonetheless, they are similar when it comes to the total annual premium or expected total annual cost.

Fully insured plans break down a premium into three basic categories: reserves, fixed costs, and claims. In a fully insured arrangement, you actually prepay the fixed costs, reserves, and claim costs — you pre-fund and pay everything up to the premium level monthly based upon your enrollment, which ultimately meets the total cost expectation that the underwriter estimated for the year.

Reserves are required by law. They are the amount of money the insurance company keeps on their books to pay for claims that are incurred prior to termination, but come in their door for payment after you've terminated their contract. The companies earn tax-free interest on this money and usually charge an increase in reserves every year based on their expectations of your future claim costs.

Fixed costs include the cost of doing business: administration, taxes, profit margins, commissions, etc. Each of these amounts are included into your premium and prepaid every month.

Claim costs are the amount that the underwriter expects your group to incur throughout the year. These are based on an *incurred basis*, meaning that the plan covers those claims that are incurred while the policies are in force. This is also why reserves are required for claims that run out after termination. Claims during the runout period are covered claims under the contract.

Underwriters also include the premium cost of stop-loss in the plan (yes, they too have stop-loss coverage) because insurance companies don't take all the risk on your plan for all employees and dependents for the entire year. They push off claims that exceed a certain threshold — sometimes referred to as the *pooling point* — to a reinsurer. The pooling point might be $50,000 for one group, depending on its size, and $100,000 or more for another group. This means that only the claims under the pooling point are allocated to the actual claims experience and loss ratio for the group. Everything above and beyond that amount is forgiven in the group's claim experience, because the insurance company has ceded the excess to a reinsurer and included a small premium in your fixed costs for that coverage.

An underwriter won't price the premium too low because it could ultimately produce a less than satisfactory loss ratio. Remember, insurance companies are still in the business to make a profit, and in a fully insured arrangement any unused claims after the end of the year and the runout period are retained by the insurance company. They're not given back to the employer — they are forfeited.

Partially self-funded plans (bundled and unbundled) are calculated in much the same way, except the components are broken out and paid for separately. Specific and aggregate stop-loss premiums are paid to the reinsurer for their policy. Administrative fees paid to the administrator are for just those selected services. The employer retains all the reserves and can either fund the reserves in their own account or simply accrue for them — nothing is prepaid to an insurance company or administrator.

Claim costs are determined much in the same way as a fully insured, i.e., there is a pooling point called the specific deductible, and overall level of claims liability called an aggregate attachment point. The aggregate attachment point is the maximum claim cost that any employer could pay in any given year. It's based upon 125% of expected claims and while not impossible, it's unlikely that an employer will hit the aggregate.

The beauty of the partially self-funded plan is that the employer controls their costs by having lower premiums for stop-loss, lower administrative fees, no requirement to give reserves to the insurance company, and they only pay claims if and when the claims are incurred — nothing is prepaid. The employer has a significant cash flow benefit.

Having been in the business for 40 years and having assembled these type of plans hundreds of times, there are many ways to utilize Best-in-Class vendors, plans, and programs, and also have favorable tax consequences. It's extremely important that programs are put together the right way with the right vendors. I cannot begin to tell you how many times I have talked to employers who told me that they had a bad experience in the past with self-funding and refused to again consider it. My opinion is that this may have happened because the plan wasn't assembled properly, or the broker gave bad advice, or the broker gave an inaccurate description of the plan and how it works, or the employer didn't accrue the funds necessary to pay the expenses each month.

You don't know what you don't know. You have to take the advice of someone you know and trust and who knows how to assemble the program the right way. If a broker or an agency doesn't do this on a daily basis, and has only a few partially self-funded clients, it can be problematic. They may not know Best-in-Class vendors, and this can have an adverse effect on employees and the employer. They may not have disclosed the complete and accurate information to an underwriter when quoting and/or they may be selecting various vendor programs that are laced with higher fees and commissions rather than top-shelf services.

As stated previously, most brokers and agencies have their preferred vendors. These don't necessarily include Best-in-Class vendors. The brokers may be compensated in a certain way, so the broker has a loyalty to that vendor because of a personal relationship, and/or service rendered. This doesn't mean that the client is necessarily getting the best service, or the best product, or the best program. When it comes to these products and programs, it's extremely important to ask for references and follow through on them. Don't think for a minute that everyone has a great experience just because the broker has recommended a particular company or program to you.

ANOTHER ITEM ASSOCIATED WITH MARKETING is when an insurance company markets directly to employer groups. This marketing comes from insurance companies and other vendors who approach, and try to sell directly to, employers. Again, they market the programs that they want to sell, not necessarily the ones that employers want to buy.

The conflict comes in when the insurance company is asked, "Are you a wholesaler or retailer?" In other words, as a broker, am I competing against an insurance company who markets directly to the employer (retailer), or do you want me to sell your products to my clients (wholesaler)? Am I competing with you or working with you?

Employers can deal directly with an insurance company and

other vendors, but buyer beware — you want to make sure that you're purchasing the programs and products that you have researched and studied, and have deemed them appropriate for your business, not just ones that sound appealing or for which the price is right. You may not know what else is out there, or if these programs are legitimate and proven.

There been many cases where I have had my clients deal directly with a stop-loss carrier, administrator, PBM, etc. with no additional fees or commissions attached. The employer may be paying a fee to me, but there are no additional fees from dealing with vendors directly.

A perfect example of this is where an employer may utilize a broker to investigate various programs and products, but wants to have a direct relationship with those vendors. You don't necessarily need a broker to place insurance. A broker is simply a distribution source for the insurance company. An employer can go directly to that insurance company, but you must take care that you've thoroughly vetted everything and are getting exactly what you want — and you must also make sure you know what you're paying for. Otherwise, an insurance company may be taking advantage of you and artificially inflating your premiums, or providing you with something that's not necessary.

Take care to explore all options and opportunities and make sure the employer can go directly to the insurance company with a great deal of confidence and assurance about what will be provided and at what cost.

REPORTING

REPORTING IS THE KEY TO accountability for your plan. It's important for your broker to provide a variety of reporting services and present them in a useful, understandable fashion. A lot of information that comes from Claims Administrators or an insurance company is presented in a way that illustrates what they want illustrated, or in a way that is simply produced by their claim system. In these cases, the information may or may not be presented in a fashion that summarizes all the activity for accounting, finance, or a CFO.

Insurance companies' fully insured and/or partially self-funded reporting packages typically illustrate month-to- month claims, claims year-to-date, monthly enrollment, and other general activity within plan utilization. However, it could be misleading in that it may *not* include fixed costs or other expenses *not* associated with claims. Remember — there are three components to your premium dollars: fixed costs, reserves, and claims.

Usually only the claim dollars are illustrated in reports as an expense. When the insurance company illustrates a loss ratio, they should include all premiums to claims, in addition to fixed costs — otherwise it can be misleading.

On the other hand, a Third-Party Administrator will show the same monthly claims activity. They may or may not show stop-loss premiums, or admin fees, etc. How a TPA presents (or does not present) stop-loss premiums and/ or reimbursements dictates whether or not the appropriate, equivalent premiums are illustrated.

In some cases, a TPA will simply provide an 'advise to pay' for the stop-loss premium, meaning that, based on eligibility, the amount of overall premium is provided to the client, and the client then pays the stop-loss carrier directly. In other cases, the TPA may collect the premium and remit it to the stop-loss carrier, but buyer beware: you better make sure that the TPA is submitting those premiums accurately and in a timely manner. If someone at the TPA responsible for that procedure goes on medical leave, vacation, etc. there should be someone to take their place to make sure your premiums are paid on time to the carrier.

Years ago, I worked with a particular TPA that was not remitting the premium in a timely manner and the employer was notified that their stop-loss was being canceled. It's not easy to reinstate stop-loss, particularly when you have a large claim outstanding. The policyholder, not the TPA, is responsible for the timely remittance of their premium. Separation of duties can eliminate this potential problem.

An agency should report all expenses in concise and thorough monthly reports. By month, this would include the single-family enrollment; the fixed costs broken down by line of expense — e.g., stop-loss premiums, administrative fees, PPO fees, etc.; the claims broken down by medical, dental, vision, prescription drug, etc.; as well as stop-loss reimbursements and claims applicable to the aggregate, with a loss ratio. It's a compilation of all monthly expenses in an easy "at a glance" report for your financial department. In addition, there should be detailed documents to back up and tie out the monthly summaries in the columns on the report.

IN ADDITION TO THE SIMPLE basic reports, an agency should have a sophisticated data analytics program. There are numerous data analytic companies, but it's only useful if you can provide information that's understandable and appropriate. Minimum categories that should have further breakdown of detail include:
- Executive Summary
- A membership and health plan enrollment analysis
- Employer/employee share of expenses
- Key membership metrics trending analysis
- Key Cost utilization metrics trending analysis
- Claims expense distribution
- Monthly comparison of paid claims
- Network analysis
- Prescription drug analysis
- Analysis of the top 10 providers, top 10 places of service, top 10 diagnostic groups, top 10 procedure groups, top 10 therapeutic classes of drugs

- Quality and risk measures identifying compliance to AMA guidelines and HEDIS measures
- Disease conditions utilization summary
- Preventative measures analysis
- High risk member claims analysis
- And many, many others.

YOUR INSURANCE COMPANY or TPA should be downloading the eligibility and claim files to the data analytics program on a monthly basis. It's not real time, but it comes very close. The data analytic reports ought to be usable by either you the client, or your broker to drill down on hotspots that need to be addressed and potentially changed in your plan. More about data analytics and how they can be useful in a wellness and disease management program later in the book (Chapter 7).

Obviously, it's important for an Agency to be able to generate these reports and not rely on the insurance company or TPA, because the insurance company or TPA may or may not provide their reports in a fashion and format that is usable or useful. When a broker conducts their marketing process of a prospective change in TPAs, a complete description and an example of the insurance company's or TPA's reporting package should be reviewed and studied.

There's a certain reliance on the insurance company to provide reports in a timely manner. However, a broker and their respective agency shouldn't expect that the reports from the insurance company or the TPA are the only reports to be generated for their client. Since these reports may not be complete, and/or may not necessarily provide an accurate view of the total picture, both the broker and the agency need to step up and provide their own reports to the client on a regular monthly basis.

VENDORS

VENDOR RELATIONSHIPS ARE CRITICAL TO the success of any broker and their agency. Relationships bring about the ability to study the programs that the vendor provides, and the opportunity to expose these needed programs and products to their prospects and clients. Without vendor and market relationships, an employer has limited access to all the programs, products, and policies in the space of employee benefits and health insurance.

When I refer to vendors, I am referring to many different types of companies. These include insurance companies, third-party administrators, reinsurers, pharmacy benefit managers, life and disability insurance companies, dental and vision insurance companies, supplemental benefits, and all ancillary insurance providers. They also include nontraditional insurance company relationships, including wellness vendors, prepaid legal, on-site clinics, disease management, and other miscellaneous companies. Vendors are the companies that an employer uses to provide services to the health plan.

These are typically introduced to employers by brokers and agencies, but the employer could also get to know them through direct marketing and contact. The vendors that you utilize are only as good as the research that goes into them. Your broker's knowledge of and exposure to these companies is very important. If a broker tends to place all their business with one or two insurance companies, you have limited exposure to the rest of the world.

Most of these vendor companies have marketing representatives that will call on brokers and invite them to sell their products. Obviously, if a vendor has no knowledge of the broker's existence (perhaps it's a small agency), or the broker is not in the same geographic region that the representatives cover, then there's no way for either to meet. Many vendors try to gain exposure at trade shows, seminars, and speaking engagements. Vendors tend to call on large agencies more than they would a small agency only because the larger agency has more salespeople and therefore can potentially drive more revenue to the vendor. It's logical to think that a small agency may never even have exposure to certain insurance markets and related vendors just because the broker is unaware that those vendors exist, and/or the vendor doesn't know that the small broker agency exists. A small broker, by my definition, is one that only has roughly 5 to 10 salespeople or less, in addition to other staff. It can also be measured by total premium placed and/or total revenue received.

LET'S TAKE THIRD PARTY ADMINISTRATORS for example. These are TPAs that provide services for partially self-funded plans. There are many TPAs in the country — some have a local presence, some regional, and some national. In some cases, the national TPAs are owned by or affiliated with an insurance company. An insurance company wants to "cover the waterfront" so to speak, so they may have acquired independent TPAs and pulled them in under their "umbrella." This gives them access to not only their insurance related customers and prospects, but also gives them additional exposure to those employers who want to use an "independent" TPA.

Since there are hundreds of TPAs throughout the country and they all have different geographic footprints, it's impossible for any given broker to have knowledge of all these TPAs. Some TPAs I would characterize as a Tier 1 TPA — meaning that they are superior or excellent at what they do and in the services they offer. A Tier 2 TPA might be one that provides above average to average services to their clients, and a Tier 3 would be a small TPA that provides only basic services.

Tier 1 TPAs are typically large regional or national companies. In my experience, many TPAs only gain exposure to an insurance agency of any size by either calling on the agency because the broker knows or has heard that they exist, or perhaps the broker has approached the TPA because they want to get a quote. We've already covered the quoting and marketing process, so whether that quote is actually presented to the employer is another story.

Assuming that a broker has done consistent business with any given TPA, and has had a relatively good experience with that TPA (as well as their clients), then the broker may feel that the need to go out to the marketplace and find another TPA is unnecessary. In other words, if the TPA that they are accustomed to working with is providing the services that the broker wants them to provide with great service, why would the broker necessarily go and try to find another TPA to offer similar services?

It's important to note that not all of these vendors can provide all the same services or level of services that another does; there are so many products and services with each of these vendors that they cannot possibly be the same. Many outsource no-core services and programs to other third parties. The broker may think the services are the same, or the broker may communicate to their client that the services are all the same — but they're not. Just like any other business, some vendors are better than others. Some provide more services, some provide products, and some have their own relationships with third-party vendors that they can also bring to the table. This is important to know because not every vendor can be everything to everybody.

As we use the TPA example, each TPA also has its own relationships with stop-loss carriers. These carriers are the entities that provide the reinsurance for a self-funded plan. Most TPAs have their own relationships with the stop-loss vendors that they've used over the years, are comfortable when a claim is made, and have been accustomed to working with these vendors.

However, not every TPA works with every reinsurer. There's a mutual process of approval, whereby the reinsurer has to be comfortable that the TPA is paying claims accurately, appropriately and in a timely manner; and the TPA has to be comfortable that the stop-loss carrier is going to provide their services in a timely manner when a claim occurs. It's not automatic for either entity. The point is that if a broker doesn't have additional, outside relationships with stop-loss carriers, then they will only be able to show their prospective client the stop-loss carriers that a particular TPA has relationships with — and the number of carriers will be limited.

Just like the example above, it's very, very important for a broker to have access to — and knowledge of — many vendors and their services. If you were buying a car and you only had access to Chevrolet and Ford, and only the automobiles and trucks that they offered, you would be limited with their particular interior and exterior packages, and you wouldn't have an opportunity to look at any other makes like BMW, GMC, Dodge, and Chrysler.

SEVERAL YEARS AGO, I HAD THE opportunity to provide a quote to a business and out of the 4 or 5 other brokers that were also quoting (my competitors) I was the only one that provided an extremely competitive proposal. Upon review, the employer asked me, "Why haven't I seen this before?" I told her that you're only as good as the brokers that you're dealing with. In other words, if the broker doesn't have access to — or knowledge of — a particular insurance company or other vendor, there is no possibility of you seeing that quote.

So I had gone outside the realm of "vendor knowledge" from my competitors, and was able to provide a quote much more competitive than anyone else. And it was only because of my knowledge of and relationship with that vendor.

I've also been in situations where I've approached a new prospect and they have told me that they were comfortable with their current broker, and that their broker provided them with all the quotes that they needed. My thought was, "What does that mean? You think your broker has access to *all* the competitive markets? Does your broker have a lock or knowledge on who's competitive and who isn't?" The quotes you get are only as good as the broker's access to those markets.

As outlined in a previous chapter, many vendors will typically provide quotes to brokers on a first-come, first- serve basis, or they will provide quotes to everyone who's requested them. The first-come, first-serve basis is one that actually limits the opportunity for you to see that quote. Many brokers use this opportunity as a way to block their competitors, so that while they may never intend to present this particular quote to their prospect or client, neither can their competitors.

When a vendor issues multiple quotes to multiple brokers, this can cause problems as well. If all of the data and information has not been consistently submitted to the vendor, and the vendor is providing multiple quotes with multiple rates based on inconsistent data, it creates confusion in the marketplace, and in some cases it will actually be an impediment to an underwriter because they don't know whose information to believe or trust.

Many brokers provide incomplete data, or do not provide the data that might otherwise increase rates, hoping that their quote will be more competitive and they will sell the case. At the end of the day, it will come back and haunt them because underwriters don't like to be fooled. To firm up the quote, they will still request all of the data that was not initially provided prior to the effective date, which may cause the rates to go up.

Sometimes a vendor will provide a "soft or conditional quote" because there may be too much time between the time of the quote and the effective date of the new policy. For example, a broker may go out and get quotes for their client whose plan is on a calendar year basis, but the broker may solicit quotes in July or August so that they are well ahead of their competitors and have everything assembled in a timely manner. This is good, except that an underwriter will only provide a soft quote and won't firm up the numbers until the January 1 date approaches. So while the employer is trying to make decisions based on this "soft quote," they may encounter difficulty because the underwriter will seek additional information between August and the end of the year before they will firm up their quote. This, in turn, could alter the plan changes that the client had planned based on "soft numbers".

Many of my clients in the past have moved away from a calendar year renewal simply because of this reason. They're trying to make plan design decisions, employee contribution decisions, renewal selections, HSA and FSA elections, and open enrollment all around the end of the year. Throw in holidays and employee vacations, and you've got a number of very difficult decisions to make in a short period of time.

Your plan can renew on a calendar year basis for deductibles, coinsurance, out-of-pocket, etc., but in many cases, it's better to have a stop-loss renewal in September or October, for example. This permits all of the soft numbers to become firm and effective at the beginning of the fourth quarter or sometime therein, and thus allows an employer to make all the necessary changes to their plan based on hard numbers. Open enrollment goes a lot smoother and there's no second-guessing and last minute decision-making. Many brokers think that everything has to flow with the January 1 effective date, and this is simply not the case. **You don't know what you don't know.**

LIFESTYLE RISK MANAGEMENT

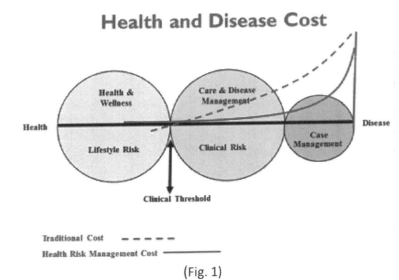

(Fig. 1)

A NUMBER OF YEARS AGO, I was a Partner and Co-Founder of a Wellness and Disease Management company. As one of my clients once said, "Wellness is so ill-defined, it's like warm Jell-O — you can never get your arms around it." And he was spot on.

Everyone has a definition of wellness; some think it's covering certain screenings and procedures at 100%, some think it's having lunch and learns, some think that it's about having activity challenges, some think it's paying a membership at the gym, Biometric screenings, and/or any combination of the above.

There are three types of people in any given organization — there are those who are well, meaning that they have no health risks or clinical conditions; there are those who have lifestyle risks such as obesity, stress, lack of nutrition and/or exercise; and there are those who have clinical risk, meaning they have a chronic medical condition and these are the ones driving claim costs.

If you look at these types of risk on a continuum (See Fig. 1), those on the left are those who are well, those in the middle have lifestyle risks, and those on the far right of the continuum are those whohave the clinical risks. As one moves from left to right, the cost of care goes up exponentially. Therefore, it's important to have a "wellness program" that tries to keep people from moving across the continuum.

Those members who are in the clinical risk category could have a number of chronic conditions or comorbidities. Because these conditions are chronic, they are not going away, and they may not necessarily improve. It's all about compliance. It's about managing compliance to AMA guidelines and HEDIS measures so that their condition doesn't worsen, and/or at least is slowed down. The program for chronic conditions should be one that can educate employees or members about their condition, and motivate them so that they have the skill sets to self-manage or self- administer their condition.

It's extremely important that the education and motivation is one that is also consistent with physician guidelines. We built a program utilizing nurse guidelines that consistently revolved around and were integrated with physician guidelines and clinical pathways. In this way, the nurse practitioner was providing information about the patient's care that was consistent with that of the medical doctor and care treatment guidelines. And, everything was consistent between nurses so that one nurse wasn't providing care that was inconsistent with another nurse providing the same care to a different member.

We were a national provider of customized and integrated riskmanagementprogramsforwellness, lifestylemanagement, and disease management. The model was designed for self- funded employers and focused on populations with 37 cost risks that could be identified.

It was a highly interactive model and delivered value to benefit employees and their families. It was a "high touch" program that resulted in high participation and included an active outreach system. We identified, monitored, and managed compliance to clinical conditions, resulting in a healthier and more productive work force and a strong return on investment to the employer.

EVERY WELLNESS PLAN SHOULD HAVE an active wellness initiative: coverage should be designed for preventative screenings and tests. It should also have a wellness committee, and wellness events should be offered to all participants. The goal is to keep the "well" well, and manage the rest.

A wellness program is a risk management program for healthcare. There are two types of risk in every plan population — clinical risk, which is what's driving your claim cost — and lifestyle risk, a precursor to clinical risk. High touch interventions through our program resulted in an average participation rate of 74%. This is in stark contrast to traditional lifestyle management and disease management programs that boast 8-12% participation.

The question is how do you identify those that are eligible for lifestyle riskmanagementand/orclinicalriskmanagement? For lifestyle risk, it is done through a health risk assessment and biometric screening. For clinical risk, it is done through access to medical and pharmaceutical claims data.

HEALTH RISK ASSESSMENTS AND BIOMETRIC SCREENINGS

HEALTH RISK ASSESSMENTS (HRAS) and biometric screenings are used to identify individuals that are eligible for lifestyle management. These tests ask questions related to one's habits, behaviors, and lifestyle. The biometric screening identifies or searches for clinical issues such as high cholesterol and blood pressure, and body mass index (BMI). There are three types of health risk assessments: paper, Internet, and interactive voice response. You should utilize whatever is best suited for your population depending upon their access to the Internet kiosks, their educational level, and your culture.

From the HRA and biometric screening, a Personal Profile Report is developed for each individual identifying the status of their lifestyle and how it affects their health. There's also an Executive Summary which provides aggregate results for the entire participant population to the employer. This is the roadmap to the future. Our program could identify 16 different lifestyle risks including tobacco use, three or more stress signs, sedentary lifestyle, and poor nutrition.

The aim of lifestyle management is to assist those individuals that have high health risks — and good intentions to lower those risks — but lack the motivation, or don't know how to do so. Our health advisors were guided by the Prochaska "level of readiness to change" model and developed individualized risk solution programs and ongoing monitoring.

We utilized medical and pharmaceutical claims data to identify those individuals that had clinical risks. We received a rolling 24 months of data from the Claims Administrator that included every single medical and prescription drug claim that had been filed by all members covered under the plan for that period of time. Our model assigned a Risk Index based upon the nature of risk for that member over that 24-month period.

WHAT SHOULD YOU LOOK FOR IN A DISEASE MANAGEMENT PROGRAM?

A DISEASE MANAGEMENT PROGRAM should be a population- basedprogram; itshouldidentifyandmonitorupto 21 chronic conditions and focus on the top 15% of the population that drives 85% of the cost. It should also identify emerging risk and monitor clinical compliance to AMA guidelines. Effective Disease Management should not rely on self-reporting, and should also identify comorbidities through claims activity and create a virtual medical record that is updated monthly. Our program managed conditions such as asthma, hyperlipidemia, hypertension, chronic pain, congestive heart failure, COPD, diabetes, and many other conditions.

Our "Explorer" took the data from the Pharmacy Benefit Manager, the Third-Party Administrator, the Health Risk Assessment, and the biometric screening, and created integrated, patient-centric data, which could then be utilized by nurses, physicians, and pharmacists to identify, assess, and intervene with employees that were at risk.

It's much like a company that has a fleet of trucks. The trucks are running everywhere day in and day out, delivering their products to their customers. These trucks have safety and preventative maintenance programs such as tire rotation, oil change, filters, and lubing. There are serious consequences to those trucks if their maintenance needs are not attended to. Our program was like a giant GPS in the sky that could look down and manage and monitor compliance as to when those trucks were ready for any kind of maintenance.

Population risk management programs should evaluate the "risk" for every person in the health plan. On average, 20% of the plan population will have at least one diagnosed chronic condition and 75% of those are manageable through self-care.

Evidence-based guidelines are critical to the success of the plan. Evidence-based guidelines rely on clinical guidelines that have proven results for physicians. Our plan had also integrated these guidelines with nursing self-care guidelines. This enabled us to standardize nursing practices and target specific deficits. It also translated into a long-term clinical intervention and tracking program that we utilized called Nurse Navigator. By contrast, if nurses were using an inquiry assessment approach (self reporting) and advice based on general knowledge, it would create inconsistent outcomes.

A tracking system is a must for documenting all activity associated with a member. While there are many explanations companies give as to how they track activity, you have to dive deep into how a wellness and Disease Management company actuallyoperates. This is certainlythecasewhenyouhaveactive interventions with members. It's important to understand how initial contact is made; how often, how frequently and by what method ongoing discussions are initiated; and what frequency is tracked and what their definition of it is. Are they using registered nurses? Are they using LPNs, or other staff people who don't have a clinical background?

The objective is to educate and motivate individuals to make changes that will improve their conditions and allow them to become clinically compliant through self-care. It was a differentiated solution, an integrated program. It was a population-based program that utilized a data analytics tool to identify, monitor, and manage clinical compliance. It utilized evidence-based guidelines for nurses and created very high participation rates. The results over a 2 ½ year period are below:

- Office Visits Per 1,000 Members were reduced by 14.5%
- Emergency Room Visits per 1,000 Members were reduced by 39.1%
- Admissions Per 1,000 Members were reduced by 25.5%

• Cost Per Member Per Year was reduced by 15.3%

HOW DO YOU DRIVE COMPLIANCE AND PARTICIPATION?

WHEN A MEMBER IS IN compliance for their particular health condition and meets all the plan requirements, then they become eligible for a reward. Since these programs are voluntary, it's important to provide the right program for members to access as well as a reward that is consistent with your culture, but is also significant enough to attract member participation.

There are many types of rewards that members flock to, and that could include everything from cash to tangible items to days off to gift certificates to lower deductibles and/or contributions out of their paycheck. Every group is different and requires a different reward based on the plan's design.

How do you get started? First, adopt a commitment in your plan. Next, create a multi-year strategic plan and design rewards for participation and compliance — this can be done through either the carrot or the stick. And lastly, develop an effective communication plan and implementation timeline.

THE DEFINITION OF INSANITY

ALBERT EINSTEIN AUTHORED THE DEFINITION of insanity: "doing the same thing over and over and expecting different results." This is so true in the world of health-care plans — and it drives me nuts.

Insanity can come from two sources: the broker and/ or the employer. In most cases, the employer simply follows what the broker recommends, which in many cases is clearly insanity, because the broker doesn't know any different — yet they keep doing the same things over and over.

This usually starts when a group gets a less-than-desirable rate increase at renewal, or the service from the insurance company or administrator is so bad that alternatives must be explored. Most brokers don't really get to the root cause of an unfavorable renewal increase, because they may see it as the edict of an underwriter with little or no room to negotiate. So now the insanity begins.

Insanity can generally take two different, but consistent forms — either change the vendor (insurance company, TPA, stop-loss, etc.) or change the plan of benefits by shifting the cost to employees through higher deductibles, copays, out of pocket exposures, etc. Granted, sometimes these changes are necessary for the rates to be competitive and consistent in the marketplace, or if service becomes an issue, or if there are network changes — any number of reasons — but the frequency of change in stop-loss carriers or the change from one insurance company to another each year is incredible.

Just ask an underwriter how busy they are three months prior to a group's renewal, predominantly calendar-year renewals. Roughly 70% of all health plans renew on a calendar year basis in the U.S., so the 4th quarter of the year is total chaos for insurance company underwriters and related vendors, because of brokers who want to seek insurance product alternatives.

A company typically changes vendors because of price increases. The broker perspective that is communicated to the employer is, "Let's go find something cheaper." While premium increases occur with regularity and many times are unacceptable and require change, the broker needs to 'look under the hood' to determine and understand the root cause of the problems so they can recommend corrections — they should not simply move business from one carrier to another and expect different results!

THE SECOND FORM OF INSANITY comes from changing the actual plan of benefits. The thought is that cost-shifting benefits to employees will somehow lead to lower, long-term healthcare costs. While increasing the deductibles, copays, and out-of- pocket limits may initially lower premiums, it's a short-term solution to a long-term problem. It doesn't lower the cost of healthcare — it simply shifts the cost to employees.

While one could argue the benefits of High Deductible Health Plans create a more consumeristic and educational approach to the use of our healthcare system, I could also argue that they create a habit of neglecting needed services, screenings, prescriptions, etc. due to the greater expense that has been shifted to the employees.

Cost shifting to employees does lower the healthcare expense to the employer — everyone knows that — either through lower premiums, higher employee contributions, or perhaps immediate or short-term claim costs. However, this doesn't solve the real, long-term problem of increasing healthcare costs.

In order to avoid the "insanity" in healthcare, one must look into the root causes of the group's healthcare expense. Is it because of chronic conditions? Acute, high-cost claims? High facility costs? Expensive drugs? Data — the *right* data — is key to this investigation, and having someone who can interpret the data and recommend innovative, effective, and proven solutions is critical.

It seems that brokers and employers always focus on the *price* of a plan-the premiums. If they don't like the *price* of the plan they go out and shop it with other companies, always looking for a better *price*. This is true for fully insured plans as well as self-funded programs. Who can be our TPA for a lower price? Who can beat the renewal of the incumbent carrier? What network has a lower access fee?

At the end of the day, it's not about price — it's about cost.

Cost reflects prices within the plan, but also reflects the value that is brought to the table by those vendors associated with the plan. In other words, what good is a low price for a TPA if they don't have or utilize capabilities to manage eligibility or claims? What value does a low premium have if a carrier is buying the business, or has an incomplete network?

I have implemented programs whereby the price for a service or stop-loss might have been slightly higher than a competitor, but the value that comes with that service has had a tremendous effect on the outcomes and lowered their overall costs significantly more than what the cheaper plan would have.

With regard to the healthcare benefits you provide to employees, it's not about price — it's about cost. There is a difference.

YOU THINK YOUR BROKER IS DOING A GOOD JOB...

THROUGHOUT MY CAREER, I HAVE ALWAYS BEEN amazed at how great ideas and prospective clients do not seriously consider proven strategies because the ideas were not presented by their broker.

An insurance broker, by definition, is one who places insurance — they *are* the distribution source for insurance companies. They search the market on behalf of their clients, looking for the lowest price they can find. They are "transactional" by nature and they are paid commissions for placing insurance with any given company. They also get a pay raise through a larger commission every time their clients' premiums go up at renewal.

I recently had the opportunity to consult with a Public Entity about their health plan and what opportunities could be explored to lower their costs — without that cost shifting to the employees. Their costs were already approaching the Cadillac Tax levels and rising. Admittedly, the group was reluctant to talk to me because they felt their broker was doing a "good job." Really?

Most employers don't have any real, specific expectations of their broker — except, perhaps, to help employees with a claim, assist with an administrative billing issue, quote different health plans with different deductibles, or educate the employer and employees on the benefits of an HSA or HRA. Anything outside the broker's comfort zone gets deferred to the insurance company or Claims Administrator.

After reviewing my findings with the Finance Director and members of the company's "Insurance Committee", I was confident that the amount that the group would save was significant enough for them to proceed over the next couple of years and begin to implement strategies to dramatically lower their costs by almost 33%! I couldn't have been more wrong!

Instead, they told me that they decided to do nothing and would stay the course with their current program and broker.

In the meantime, they actually went to their broker and asked what they could do to lower their costs. This insurance broker was the one who had put them with their current plan, providers, and vendors; the one who had recommended their current benefits to employees and had created their employee contributions — clearly the one who had already "done everything" they knew to lower their costs. Wouldn't you think that if the broker had any knowledge of additional programs to assist the Public Entity, they would have already offered these programs to their client? At least I'll give them the benefit of the doubt and think that they would   have.

The reality is that their broker had no knowledge of these programs until the Public Entity gave their broker some ideas about my recommendations and asked what their broker could do. And the Entity thinks their broker is doing a "good job"? And the broker is paid a handsome sum for doing a "good job"?

Several things are disturbing about this situation:
- Taxpayers would be — and should be — irate at the historic, excessive costs that have needlessly been absorbed by the Entity and recommended by their broker.
- The employees and staff, having such high deductibles and high contributions, would be furious to know that the Finance Director and Insurance Committee hadn't done something sooner, or on my recommendations, to reduce their costs — especially continuing to employ the same broker who has had no solutions.
- The Entity may not have kept my information confidential, as requested. However, if their trusted broker is so good, then:
- Why hadn't they recommended programs before so that the Entity didn't have the escalating costs that they do?
- Why did their broker only "wake up" and react when their client asked them for ideas?
- Instead of researching alternative programs and understanding the implications of the programs they installed for the Entity, why did the broker rely on the insurance company and administrator to implement their programs at the expense of the Entity with no knowledge, oversight, or scrutiny?

- Will the broker have trouble implementing the actual programs I recommended due to lack of familiarity?
- And lastly, in my opinion, shouldn't a broker only get paid when they bring solutions to their clients — not more commissions when their clients get a rate increase?

I can only try to imagine why the Entity stays loyal to this broker — there are all kinds of things that could be going on, above or under the table. But one thing is for sure: the Entity's trusted broker — the one who is doing a "good job" — will certainly have a tough time finding solutions that are foreign to them. That's because they rely on the insurance companies and Claims Administrators to bring solutions — they have very few of their own that affect COST.

The Entity shouldn't be so convinced and closed-minded about how "good" their broker really is. Or, maybe it's all just sour grapes on my part.

FINANCIAL INCENTIVES FOR YOUR HEALTHCARE TEAM?

I RECENTLY CONDUCTED A HEALTHCARE innovations seminar on "How To Reduce Your Healthcare Costs — Without Changing Benefits For Employees." It was well attended by Unions, as well as both public and private sector employers.

The topics included programs related to Reference-Based Pricing and the steps to take to implement such a program, how to be prepared in the event of an ACA DOL Audit, cyber-security, and the benefits, costs, and ROI of On-Site and Near-Site clinics.

During one of the presentations, one of the speakers asked the audience a very interesting question: "Who on your healthcare team has a financial incentive to make your costs go down?" Your healthcare team can include many players: your Insurance Company, Third Party Administrator, Reinsurance Company, hospitals, doctors, Pharmacy Benefit Managers, Networks, and perhaps your broker or consultant as well.

When you think about it, none of them have a financial incentive to lower your costs! In fact, they all have a financial incentive and benefit if your costs go up! And they actually have the control and ability to make them go up!

Employers are in a very disturbing position when it comes to healthcare costs for their employees. We've come to a point in time where the costs have become so high that offering meaningful benefits to employees is going to become unsustainable — particularly if costs continue to rise at these alarming rates. There are many reasons why costs continue to increase, which has been the subject of previous blogs. I have also mentioned several techniques that could be implemented and utilized that can actually lower overall costs as well — without changing or reducing benefits to employees.

When you apply the **Rule of 72** to your healthcare costs (insurance premiums, claim costs, prescription drugs, etc.) it will become too expensive for employers to continue to offer benefits that will attract and retain employees. For most businesses, healthcare costs can be second in company expenses only to payroll.

An employer should investigate and explore techniques that will not only reduce the rate of increase, but will actually lower costs. With many programs, this can be done easily through an audit of your current health insurance program, regardless of whether you are self-funded or fully insured. Data and contracts from your plan are needed, but it can be an effective method to understand and identify compelling financial opportunities within your plan, without taking a **Leap of Faith**. Doing the same thing over and over (changing insurance companies, TPAs, and cost shifting to employees) and expecting a different result — which is the **Definition of Insanity** — will not produce the necessary long-term reductions in costs. It's simply hoping that another change will somehow affect the health of employees, hoping for bigger discounts, hoping that somehow your prescription drug costs will go down, and so on. The reality is that it's not changing any of this.

A deep dive into your plan is necessary to get a handle on where things are out of control and what can be done to affect and lower them for the long haul.

BUNDLED VS. UNBUNDLED

A LOT OF PEOPLE ASK ME what it is that I do. I could go on and on about what I do, but it's best summarized by telling them, "I try to get people to do what they don't want to do," and they ask, "What's that?"

I say, "Change."

I'm a healthcare consultant that works with specific employers who have partially self-funded their health plan benefits for employees. For this discussion, I use the term partially self-funded and self-funded synonymously. Unless you're over 1,000 or 2,000 employees, you're always going to be partially self-funded when utilizing stop-loss reinsurance.

When I was a kid I used to ride the bus after school over to my grandparents' house and help them in the yard raking leaves, mowing the lawn, washing windows, and the like. When I got done working, I would inevitably go inside the house and watch TV, waiting for one of my parents to come and pick me up and take me home for dinner.

Back then, the TV was built into a Hi-Fi Console — a large, credenza-like piece of furniture with the TV built into the middle of it. The speakers were also built into the cabinet, on the top left side there was a turntable, and on the top of the right side there was a tuner and AM/FM radio. This was all built into one big, heavy piece of furniture.

One day I was over there and went inside, waiting for my parents after working, and the Hi-Fi was gone. I asked my grandma what had happened and she said it had blown a tube or something and Grandpa had ordered another one. So a time or two later I went back to do more work and when I went inside after working, there was a brand-new Hi-Fi, only this time it was a maple cabinet instead of oak, but everything was still all built in.

We all know they don't make those anymore and people have their entertainment system built through components. They may have a Sony TV, a JVC receiver, Infinity speakers, etc. Everything is built and assembled through components.

The beauty of this is that when one of the components goes bad or you choose to add another component, you can do so without changing the integrity of the entertainment system.

What I do is build health plans through components. If you're contracted with an insurance company, then you have the Hi-Fi console. Everything they provide is under their roof. For example, if you're with Blue Cross then they are providing the administration, it's their reserves, it's their network, it's their pharmacy — they provide everything. So if you get a renewal increase that you don't like, you either go find another Hi-Fi or pay the increase. You have to change everything.

With a health plan that is built through Best-in-Class components, if one of the components goes bad you only have to replace that component, not the entire Hi-Fi. For example, if you get an increase in stop-loss, you simply go out and shop for new stop-loss and it's invisible to employees. You don't have to change the ID cards, the benefits, the pharmacy, the administration, etc.

It's important for your broker to know how to put together an entertainment system for healthcare. And it's extremely important that your broker knows not only which components to put together, but also which companies/ vendors in the marketplace offer Best-in-Class components.

RFP WRITING

ONE O THE ESSENTIAL REQUIRED SERVICES for a client that a broker should perform is that of writing a Request For Proposals (RFP). This questionnaire and inquiry could go to a variety of vendors for proposed services and could include a Third Party Administrator (TPA), a Pharmacy Benefit Manager (PBM), a reinsurer, a Wellness and Disease Management company, etc. And while this is an essential service offered by a broker for their client, the question that comes in to play is: "Is the RFP constructed in a thorough and effective manner?" In other words, are all the essential items that need to be discovered and evaluated included in the RFP in the precise and proper way?

Brokers have a tendency to have favorite markets for all of the vendors mentioned above. They may or may not be aware of alternative markets simply because of their geographic reach or experience. While the actual RFP questionnaires are assembled, it's very important that the RFPs be delivered to a wide cast of markets so that the client gets the best results. If a particular RFP is simply a copy-and-paste type of document, then it's not constructed in such a way that best serves the client and their specific needs and objectives. Unfortunately, it's simply a document that's been utilized many times before and is rather generic. If a broker is working strictly on behalf of the client, the RFP should reflect very specific needs and objectives of the client, not dozens of group of employers before them.

Most RFPs are sent out to various vendors to evaluate their services and prices — after all, it's a request for proposal. I would argue that an RFP is, in many cases, inadequate to understand a vendor's capabilities. Rather, a Request For Information (RFI) is more suitable to understand the vendor's exact capabilities, and once again, the exact, precise, and thorough questions need to be asked. You can negotiate price, but you cannot negotiate capabilities.

For example, I have talked with various Third-Party Administrators (TPAs) who say they have seen RFPs that have been sent to them by a broker where it's very, very obvious by the nature of the questions that the RFP is designed to obtain the best response from a competitor vendor. The RFP may be designed for an insurance company yet sent to the TPA. It may ask questions that are relevant to the insurance company, but not the TPA. On the other hand, questions could be just the opposite.

When a broker writes an RFP, it should be a customized document that includes all aspects of the request for information and capabilities regardless of the administrator. If more than one RFP needs to go out to accomplish this, then each RFP should be written separately for an insurance company and/or TPA.

Writing and submitting RFPs is not a matter of copy and paste. It needs to be a serious, thorough document that an employer or client can rely on to understand the capabilities of the vendor that they're evaluating and should reflect exactly what they are looking for.

As a former broker, I remember getting all types of RFPs directly from employers that sometimes asked completely irrelevant questions. It was very obvious that they too had copied and pasted questions from other RFPs simply to go through the exercise of sending them out, but did not really have a desire to make any change with their current broker.

I have seen RFPs with questions that are several pages, and RFPs that are a simple paragraph. Public sector RFPs are different from the private sector, and each vendor is different. If your broker is writing a RFP for you, make sure you ask to see it.

EXCESSIVE PHARMACY COSTS

I RECENTLY WROTE AN ARTICLE on Prescription Drug spending and Pharmacy Benefit Managers (PBM) and where brokers fit into the marketing and selection process of a PBM for their clients. I had the opportunity to actually work with another employer and examine their prescription drug program and costs. What I found out about their drug spending — and how much money this group had spent on behalf of their employees only to discover that other entities had prospered from it — is remarkable.

This employer is probably typical of most mid-sized, partially self-funded employers in the U.S. Their plan is unbundled, i.e., they utilize a large Third Party Administrator (TPA), a regional PPO network, stop-loss, and an independent PBM (although I'm not sure who selected the PBM — their broker, the TPA, or another related vendor). Their drug spending for their company employees — approximately 235 people — was approximately $626,500 in a 12-month period or $2,666 per employee per year.

I actually received their claims data and was able to reprice each prescription claim with a different PBM — one that relied on transparency and the lowest ingredient costs. The repricing assumed the exact same drug (no substitutions), the same dosage and the same quantity. The savings were over $103,000! How can this be?

As I mentioned in a previous chapter, PBMs make money in a variety of ways — spread pricing, fees, and rebates, to name a few. In this case, the profit to the PBM at the expense of the client was exorbitant, and the employer didn't know any different. Someone recommended this PBM to the employer, and the employer trusted that the PBM was competitive based on that recommendation. What the employer didn't know was that a portion of their costs was not only an extraordinary profit to the PBM, but also to other third parties. Without transparency and disclosure, how would the employer have known?

As a former broker, I have been in situations where PBMs

have repeatedly asked me, "How much of the rebate do you and the insurance agency desire?" The PBM would keep some of the rebate, pay the agency some of it, and pay the remaining rebate to the client. The PBM would charge dispensing and administration fees to the client, and keep the spread between what they purchase the drug for and what they would charge the client.

It's extremely important to ask the right questions and have a basic understanding of the PBM that you are implementing. It's equally important to know that your broker and/or TPA is aligned with the best PBM available to you and not because being compensated by that PBM serves as an incentive. It's not about how big their network is; it's about the elements that you don't necessarily consider or know about. You broker should be knowledgeable and examine these elements, but more often than not they don't do so. For a small — to medium-sized company, the differences can be extraordinary.

PROVIDER NEGOTIATION

THE DIFFERENCE BETWEEN THE RELATIONSHIP that insurance companies and their respective PPO networks or provider networks have with brokers and what brokers tend to admit is interesting. Insurance companies are notorious for saying their network is the largest, with the greatest number of providers, and the best discounts on the planet. Every network seems to suggest the same thing.

Most brokers tend to acknowledge and agree with this. This is because most brokers are unable to delve into enough detail to question these statements or understand which PPO network is in fact the best. The contracts that providers (hospitals, facilities, and physicians, etc.) have with the PPO networks are confidential. This means that the PPO cannot substantiate their remarks that they have the best discounts or the most providers. Brokers will just take them for their word.

To illustrate the point, a hospital has what is called a charge master — this is a voluminous file of all services that they render to a patient when they walk in the door and all related prices. It includes everything from Band-Aids and ibuprofen, to minutes in the operating room, to the intensive care unit, and everything in between. As you can imagine, it is substantial. These are the billed charges that all PPO discounts relate to. So when a network negotiates with a particular hospital, the discounts that they've negotiated are applied to those billed charges.

For example, a 20% discount would be the discount off the billed charges. The problem is that there are no regulations, rules, or laws that prevent the hospital from increasing their prices in the charge master. It's much like the discount that you receive at a retail clothing store when a big sale goes on. They advertise the big discount, but the store marks up the price of the clothing from what it was prior to the sale — so in reality, a bigger discount doesn't necessarily mean a lower price.

An exception to this would be where a network has negotiated a case rate on specific procedures, or a rate based on a percentage of Medicare. With most PPO networks, the Medicare plus rate only extends to charges that are below   a specific threshold — for example, $80,000 or $100,000. Anything in excess of that reverts back to a discount, off-the- bill charge. But those are the charges for which you want a better Medicare plus rate — not the smaller ones. Clearly, the facility only wants a discount across the board.

Physicians on the other hand are slightly different, yet similar. Physicians may operate and negotiate independently, or as a group of physicians, or as an association. There are many models associated with this for establishing pricing with the PPO, but usually it's a matter of two different types of pricing at the end of the day. One may be a discount off of Reasonable and Customary charges, and another might be on a Resource-Based Relative Value Scale "RBRVS". This is very similar to the Medicare plus arrangement for a hospital or facility. RBRVS is tied to Medicare, and, generally speaking, the provider would get a percentage above Medicare, e.g., 165%, 180%, 200%, etc.

The location of the providers, the number of members that an insurance company or PPO network can deliver to the providers, and other factors will dictate which methods are used. If more members can be driven to the network providers, there is usually a more aggressive pricing structure.

BROKERS WILL TEND TO BELIEVE the insurance companies or networks as to who has the best discounts. At the end of the day, the broker needs to have access to mechanisms that may substantiate those pricing structures. If the broker doesn't have access, then an employer and the broker are simply taking a leap of faith and trusting that the insurance company or network is truthful.

Sometimes, when a broker asks for claims to be repriced — which is a pretty good way of looking at alternative networks — a network may trick the broker by illustrating their best rate at their best facility, rather than citing actual pricing at the actual facility for the actual services provided. There are tricks to the trade where a network can hide the real cost of pricing that they have negotiated. You might find an insurance company that touts the highest discounts (which may be partially true) whereby they might have the best pricing at a certain hospital, but lose all the advantage of their network with the physicians

— or vice versa. So while they may be better with a particular local hospital than their competitors are, they would lose that overall advantage and overall pricing because they weren't as competitive with the physicians.

Brokers need to understand these pricing methodologies and develop strategies for more aggressive direct pricing. Direct contracting will enable a self-funded employer to negotiate its own pricing with the more important providers in their area that treat the most of the company's employees and those employees' family members. Many providers are open to direct contracting if the employer's health plan can use better benefits to incentivize employees to go to those providers rather than other network facilities.

For example, direct contracted providers might require incentives within the plan (because of a potentially greater discount) and have the plan pay 80% coinsurance after the deductible to them; other network providers paid at 70%; and non-network paid 50% or some resemblance to this. Incentives are easy to design, but the employer must take care to design the plan so that they are on the right end of the stick. This means that if an employer is going to give an additional 10% incentive to employees to go to a particular hospital, then the additional discount over and above the traditional PPO network discount needs to be more than 10%. Otherwise, it's a lose–win situation.

If brokers don't have the ability or desire to negotiate on behalf of their clients, then their clients are pretty much stuck with the PPO discounts through the network. *You don't know what you don't know.* You think you're getting the best discounts? Really the best discounts? How do you know?

Stop-loss carriers may or may not have the ability to evaluate networks, and they need to be made aware of direct contracting that exists and the pricing. They can then price their specific stop-loss deductible premiums and their aggregate attachment points at the appropriate levels. Some stop-loss carriers are better than others at evaluating this.

Knowledgeable stop-loss carriers and underwriters will give the greatest credence to Reference-Based Pricing — but it must be at a very competitive level. If Reference-Based Pricing is available for facilities as well as physicians, this is the best of both worlds. Many brokers fail to explain the pricing of the network to the stop-loss carrier, thinking that it doesn't matter, or that every carrier can give the same relative discount in their quote. Once a particular stop-loss carrier has experience with the carved out providers, and the direct contract network, then they will be more apt to provide aggressive pricing. Results are extremely important to share with an underwriter in order to get the best pricing, and stop-loss carriers can tell you which networks not to use or which ones they don't lend any credence to.

WELLNESS PLAN
DESIGN BLACKMAIL

I WAS A COFOUNDER AND PARTNER of a Wellness and Disease Management company. With this program, we managed three types of individuals: those who were well, meaning they had no medical conditions or ailments whatsoever; those with lifestyle risks, which were those who had identified risks such as stress, lack of nutrition, lack of exercise, obesity, and smoking; and those who had clinical conditions — these were people who had any of 21 chronic conditions. Everyone in the population falls into one or more of these categories.

We designed programs that managed all three types of people to prevent them from advancing into more complicated and serious conditions. We did this through several techniques: an annual biometric screening including a venipuncture blood draw, an online health risk assessment, and data analytics. Each month, claims data from the TPA and prescription data from the PBM were downloaded into our data analytics program. Our nurses identified those individuals who were diagnosed with any one of the chronic conditions and/or taking prescriptions for a particular condition.

If people were identified in the claims data as having one or more chronic conditions or were identified as having lifestyle risks through the screening and assessment, they would be invited to join their respective programs. A nurse would then contact them and assist them with self- education, self-motivation, and self-care with which they could manage their condition. These contacts by the nurses typically occurred on a quarterly basis, but could occur more frequently if the member desired.

We also provided educational information and activities for all members of a particular employer so that everyone in each of the categories was addressed. Whether you were well and attended the activities, or you were a lifestyle risk and consulted with the nurse and participated in the activities, or you were diagnosed with one or more chronic conditions and talked with a nurse as well as participated in the activities, you received a benefit. Benefits ranged from cash and financial incentives, to days off, lower contributions in your health plan, and lower deductibles and co-pays.

This particular employer had a program that was designed to manage all three types of people and created incentives — fairly substantial incentives. The employer happened to be a hospital with several hundred employees. One day, one of our nurses came into my office and wanted to tell me about an encounter with a physician who was an employee at the hospital. She came in and said, "You won't believe what just happened."

I said, "Okay, tell me about it."

She said, "Well, I called this particular doctor and he said 'so this is my blackmail call'. I responded, 'What do you mean blackmail call?' He said, 'Well, my employer (i.e., the hospital) said that I have to talk to you on a quarterly basis in order to get my incentive, so consider this conversation over and complete.'"

While I didn't identify the individual, I did tell the employer about situation.

It goes to show you that while some programs are well intended, well received, and actually have employees that express gratitude, there are always those who, while they are not in the best of health, think they have no problems and need no help, and these are the very ones who need to be served. It's important to customize your programs to garner participation from the greatest possible percentage of employees.

Our program was very successful in producing quantifiable results that lowered healthcare costs. In doing so, we managed three types of people: those who are well, those who have lifestyle risks, and those who had chronic conditions. We designed programs to manage all three types of people so that they would not regress and develop more serious ailments.

ONE OF MY CLIENTS WAS a large automobile dealer who had designed a program that was very effective and very well received by their employees. If the employee took an annual biometric screening and blood draw, answered a written health risk assessment, and participated in the lifestyle risk management or clinical risk management programs (whichever was appropriate for them), then they received a reward. The reward consisted of a brand-new, crisp $50 bill on a quarterly basis and a dark chocolate Hershey kiss.

I always got a chuckle out of the Human Resource Manager when she would go around to employees to deliver the rewards and report the success back to me. She would go in the body shop and give out the cash and the Hershey kiss during normal business hours, and people who did not participate would walk up to those who she was giving the money to and ask them, "What was that all about?" And they would say that they were getting the cash because they were working with the wellness program. She would go to the new car showroom and do the same thing.

Year after year, participation grew exponentially. They had departmental challenges that had rewards tied to them, and great participation at their lunch and learns. Overall, they had excellent participation.

One day, I was meeting with the CFO to review their overall benefit costs — they had an unbundled, self-funded plan — and I had very good news to report because we had lowered their healthcare costs through the wellness program. When I opened with remarks about having some very good news, the CFO started laughing at me and said, "I know." I said, "What do you mean you know?" He said he knew that his costs were going down because he could see the weekly check register and the cash requests were significantly less than they were in the past.

If you design the right plan with the right elements, you can do the same thing.

Made in the USA
Lexington, KY
22 April 2017